Anna Freeman Bentley
Mobility and Grandeur

Anomie

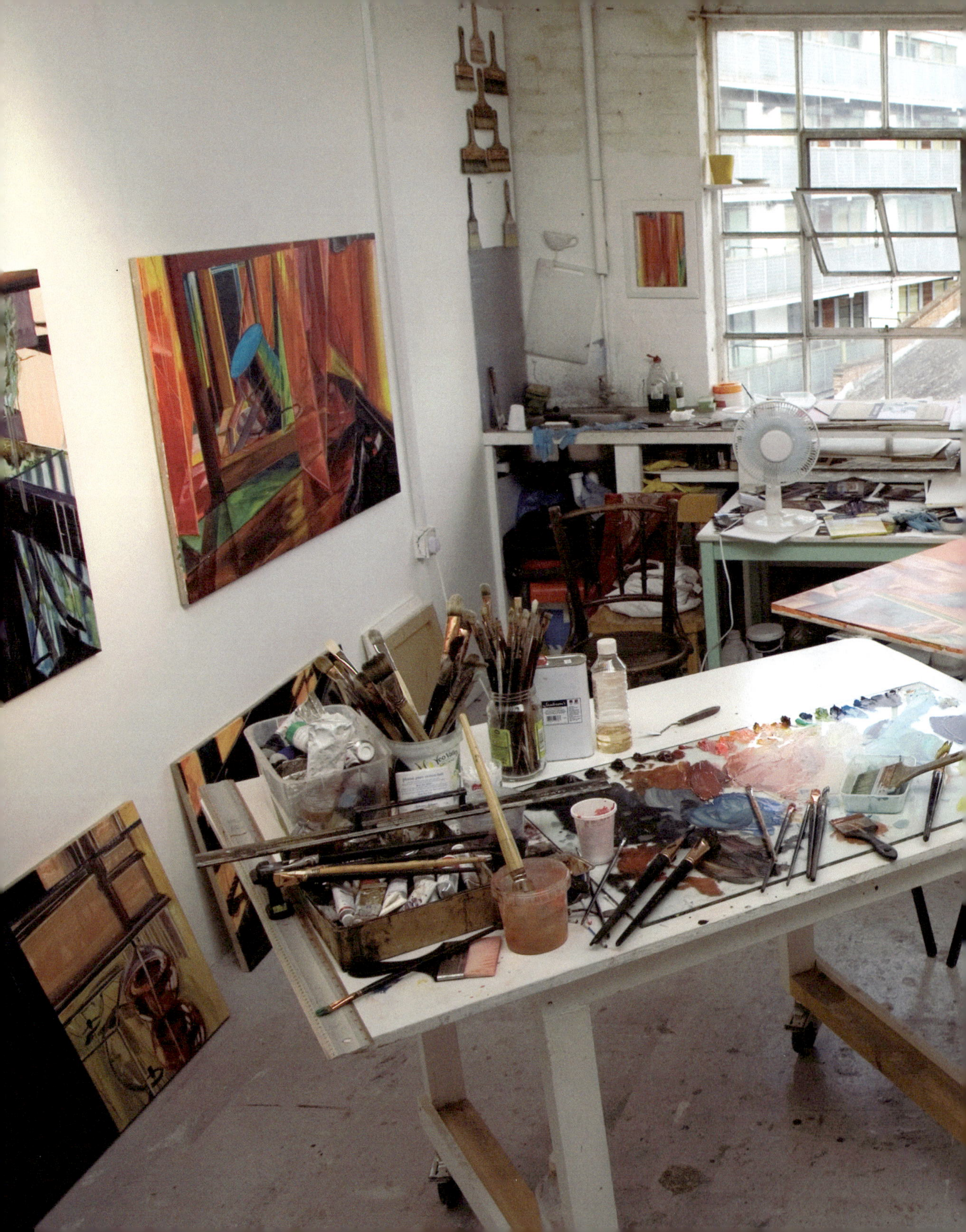

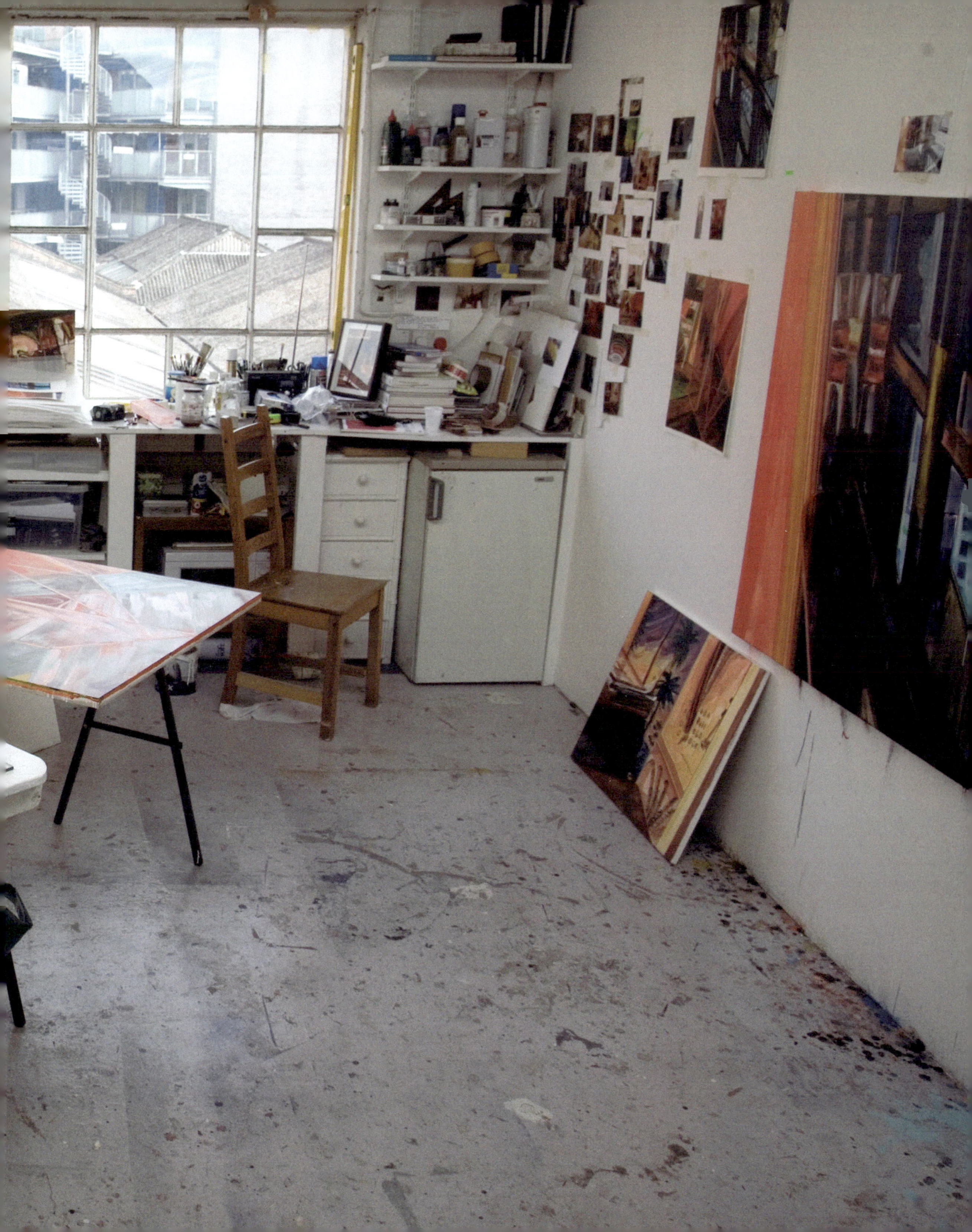

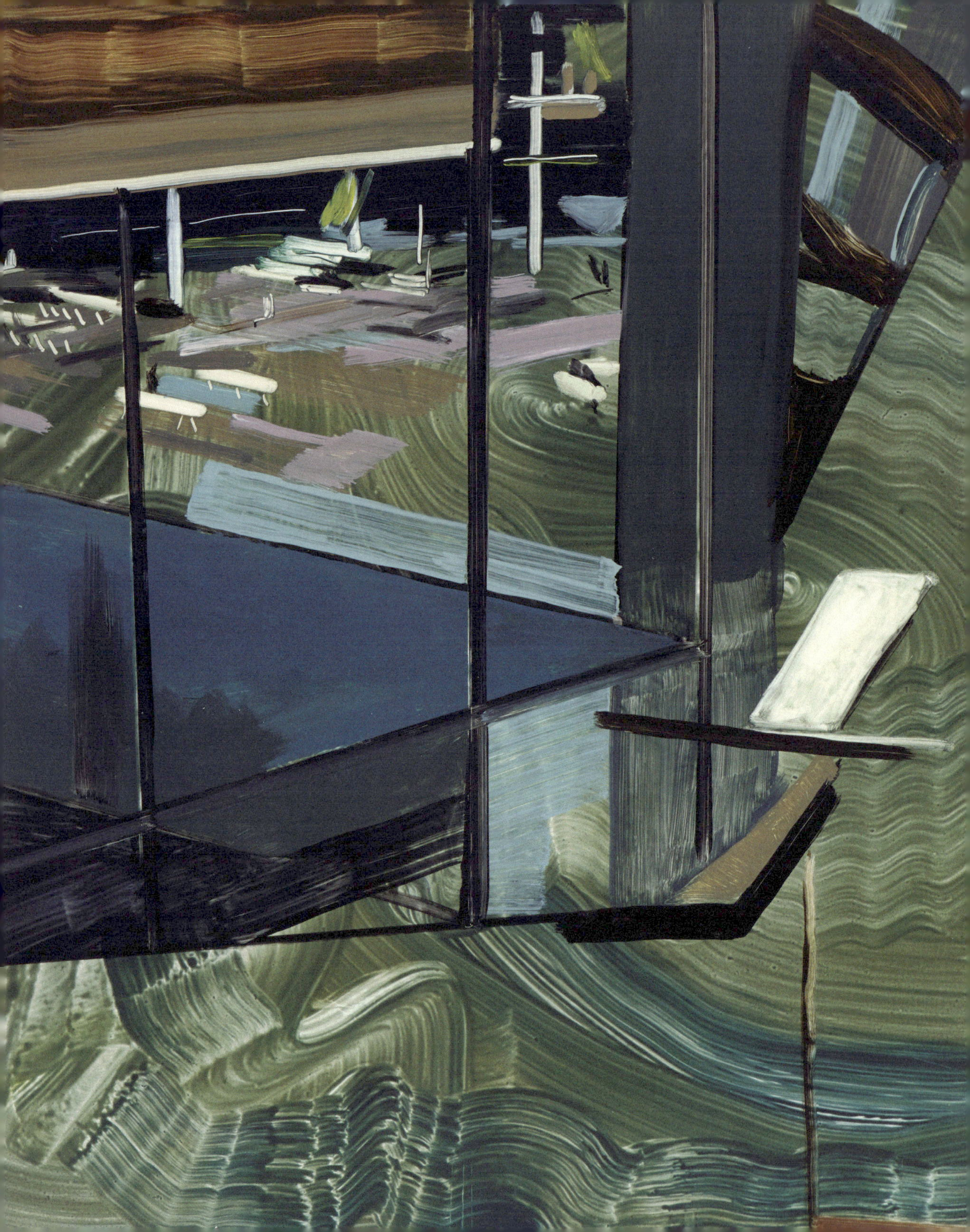

MICHELE ROBECCHI

Introduction:
Gentrifying Heterotopia

As American writer Sarah Schulman noted in her book *The Gentrification of the Mind: Witness to a Lost Imagination*, key to the logic of gentrification is the substitution of complex with simplistic realities. Mixed neighbourhoods become homogeneous, and their many languages, perspectives and experiences soon converge into a dynamic that makes them vulnerable to enforcement of conformity. When applied to a creative community, one of the consequences of this process is that infrastructural considerations are suddenly put at the top of the priority list, dramatically reducing the denizens' ability to retain, control or to shape aspects of their own daily lives, communities and environment. But it is also true that this doesn't automatically imply the establishment of a context where it's more difficult to imagine oneself as an artist. Gentrification undoubtedly allows less room for variation and even less for affordable rents and workspaces, but not necessarily for discovery or creation. Artists such as Andy Warhol or Jeff Koons are evidence that you don't need a counterculture as a playing field in order to make new, exciting art. If it is a given that interesting points of view can flourish in adversity, there is no reason to think that a potentially paralysing phenomenon like gentrification cannot also be met with imagination and oppositionality.

As a studio-resident of the London area of Hackney Wick, a post-industrial zone extensively transformed by a series of urban redevelopments culminating with the erasure of many industrial blocks and streets for the construction of the 2012 Olympic Park, Anna Freeman Bentley has witnessed first-hand the transition from a neighbourhood of relative economic and social deprivation – and simultaneously a hive of artistic production – into a destination for tourists, investment and gentrification. Although it has brought many improvements, she has also seen how mechanical and cold this transformation can be. She has observed how some of the people, companies and agencies behind these changes seem to be unaware of their own power to displace existing communities, and the many mixed agendas and kinds of ethos at play. Or, to quote Freeman Bentley's own words during my studio visit, how living and working in such conditions feels like attempting to "make somewhere home that won't let you". Coupled with her deep and long-held interest in architecture – something that since her early childhood has brought her to look at buildings and structures in an uncommonly profound way – and a research process for her art that establishes a temporary relationship with a determined site in order to make work that chronicles her experiences of it, her immersion within the gentrification of East London has resulted in a practice that addresses the changing cityscape in a way that has evolved, changed and renewed itself in a fashion not dissimilar to the process of gentrification itself.

Build Up (detail), 2013, oil on board, 40 × 52.5 cm

Characterised by titles such as *Paced*, *Spliced*, *Trace* or *View*, Freeman Bentley's recent and new paintings about gentrification follow her predilection for blurring the line between representational and non-representational images. Mirror reflections generate geometrical lines that fragment the compositions. Details of elaborately decorated floor surfaces, cocktail glasses, designer lamps and chair backs are captured and elevated to centre stage. Yet, if compared with preceding series, like the old Venetian buildings she explored in 2012, a few significant contrasts emerge. Brush marks are less watery; colours are of a different intensity; and, most poignantly, a renewed sentiment of melancholia is detectable, perhaps as much dictated by a sense of personal involvement as by anthropological drive. Similarly, the group of junk shop interiors she presented at Prague Biennale 5 in 2011, where bric-a-brac and various household goods were illustrated in a manner to emphasise their state of limbo between past and future use, suggests an emotional as well as a sociological critique. Inhabitants are ostensibly absent from her portrayal of fabricated, self-contained environments, but the psychological and political connection between the two is conspicuous. What is evident is that a significant shift has been taking place in her practice. The urban and social renovation in Hackney Wick is not something she has had to be on the lookout for or to leave her own neighbourhood to find. It is a reality that is spontaneously growing around her. These realities of regeneration and gentrification are phenomena that are reflected in other major cities around the world. Freeman Bentley's travels to, and experiences of "global" cities such as New York, Berlin, Paris and Los Angeles clearly find echoes in her explorations of her elected home city, making the underlying thrust of her work not necessarily about *a* specific city but instead using her experience of London to explore *the* contemporary city.

Interestingly, the word 'gentrification' was coined by British sociologist Ruth Glass in 1964 to denote class shifts in London neighbourhoods like Camden and Islington. Fifty years on, Freeman Bentley is continuing to explore the social, economic, political and physical manifestations of the ever-changing urban life of post-industrial East London. The London of Glass' studies was still coming to terms with the rebuilding of much of the city since World War II, though was equally still within the cycle of Britain's economic and industrial decline that came to a head in the 1970s and early 1980s, symbolised by the miners' strikes that nearly brought the country to a standstill and the government to its knees. Freeman Bentley's post-millennial London has witnessed riots and social unrest – both race and government-cuts related – in the last few years. Regeneration and gentrification have been taking place amidst destruction and protest, and Freeman Bentley has been living and working with this on her doorstep.

Rather than focus on real-life drama, however, Freeman Bentley's work captures something of the mundanity of urban renewal and gentrification. One of the things that stand out in her latest work is how a methodology sometimes adopted by artists to glorify banal aspects of everyday life seems to have been subverted to have the exact opposite outcome. Paintings like *Build Up* (2013) [p.75] or *Estranged* (2014) [p.33] almost de-glamorise the objects and places they represent. Even an atypical work like *Social* (2014) [opposite], where the elements that compose an empty café are legible in their entirety, frustrates the aspirations to grandeur of the location in question. It is interesting in this sense to analyse the liberally arranged chairs and tables in *Social* with Paul Cézanne's *The Card Players* (1894-95). Although different in style and scope, both paintings deliberately bend the fundamental rules of perspective to offer a picture lacking in loudness and drama but not in narrative and atmosphere. Whereas in *The Card*

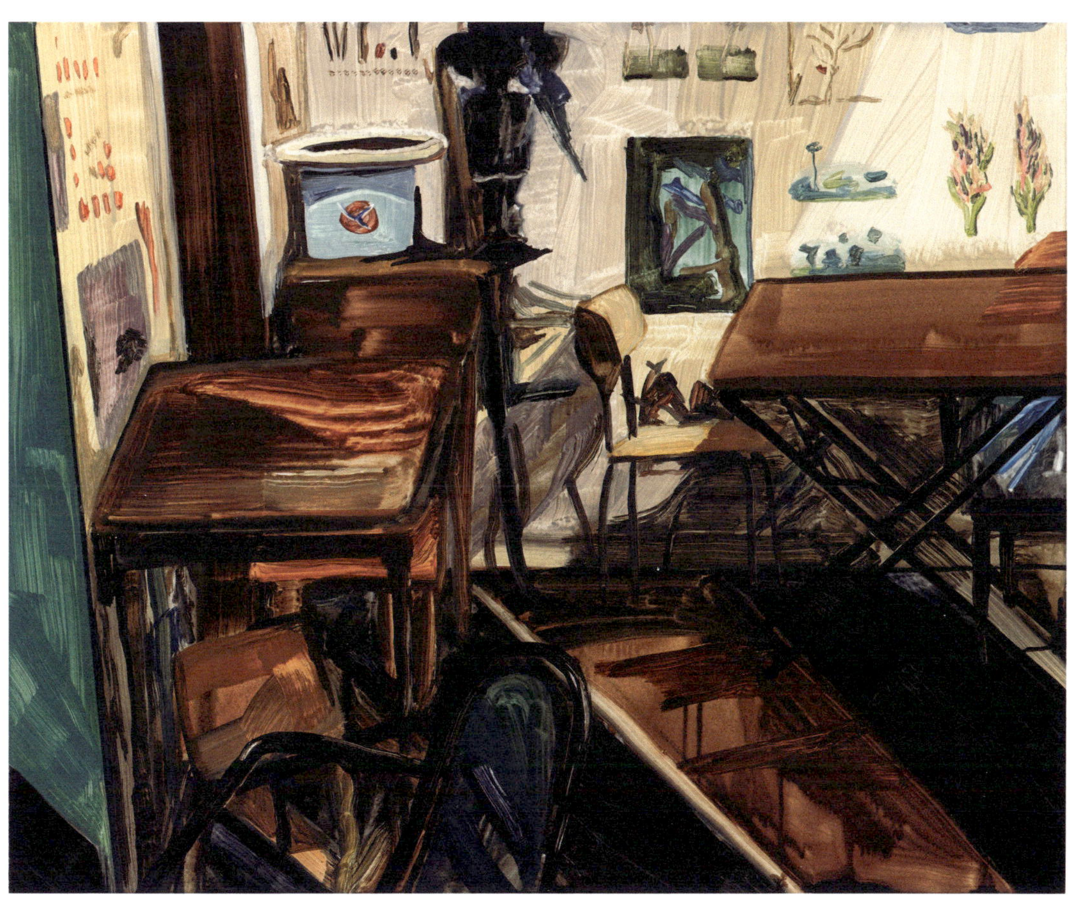

Social, 2014, oil on board, 40 × 50 cm

Players, the quiet, pensive, pipe-sucking men engaged in the game subvert the conventional image of these gatherings as rambling, rowdy affairs, in *Social* the desolated scene clashes with the bar's own ambitions, effectively suggesting one of the most striking side-effects of gentrification – that brief period of co-existence of old regulars and newcomers that makes their social gap a discernible entity. The ensuing tension is perhaps a consequence of the former, less socially and economically mobile group experiencing for the first time feelings of inadequacy when next to the latter, and it is no coincidence that Freeman Bentley's deployment of dense chromatic tones in this and other recent works resembles Michelangelo Antonioni's *Red Desert* (1964), the Italian director's first venture into the world of colour film, where a background of strongly pastel-tinted industrial buildings was used to highlight a woman's inability to come to terms with the modern world.

Social might be an exception – or a new direction – in Freeman Bentley's repertoire, but the basic ingredients that form its DNA can be sensed in more characteristic works such as the full variety of reflective surfaces in *An Awakening* (2014) [p.88], the conflicting scenarios of *Transitioning* (2013) [p.79] or the intangible, almost cubist juxtaposition of planes in *Composed of a Promise* (2013) [p.78]. The inventive use of space and light, combined with a touch of nostalgia discreetly lurking in the background makes her work mysterious enough to give viewers the possibility of building their own personal narrative. Painting, after all, is successful when it tells a story or when it provokes an emotional response, but is even more so when it captures something harder to pin down, something more ambiguous, more complex, more enigmatic. And this is certainly true of Freeman Bentley's work, in which beyond merely documenting different kinds of buildings, interiors and objects within them, she strives to capture and question the atmosphere, the mood of a place, and the effects

it has on an individual, whether psychological, emotional, or aesthetic.

Indeed, the individual's experience of and connection to architecture has been the unifying bond between all of her bodies of work to date, spanning her studies at Chelsea and the Royal College of Art through to the latest works exploring gentrified space. It is here that the variety and complexity of her brush work come into play, triggering all manner of emotive and aesthetic connections in the viewer's mind – connections between the forms, shapes, line, colour, tone, light and textures both within the artwork itself and in dialogue with how these qualities are manifest in the three-dimensional world (or fragments thereof) that they are representing. How can a painting capture things that go beyond the visual in a very literal sense, into realms where there is something deeper, or discernibly metaphysical, at work? Freeman Bentley's interests thus extend into notions of faith, belief and spirituality, into how physical space and the built environment can also be metaphors for, or manifestations of, personal journeys: interior architecture somehow mapping interior lives.

While a term such as "gentrification" is loaded with social, economic and political meaning, "regeneration" is perhaps a more fitting analogy for Freeman Bentley's painterly agenda in depicting the city – a search for betterment, renewal and improvement in the world around us. Likewise, terms such as "mobility" and "grandeur" can imply a search for personal gain, for greater wealth and status, but in Freeman Bentley's hands can serve as both a critique of such desires and aspirations, and as a metaphor for spiritual growth. Among the complex dynamics of a city such as London today, regeneration is intended to bring improvement, both to the physical environment and for the lives of those who live within it, though it is inevitably subject to many different agendas and hence is never entirely

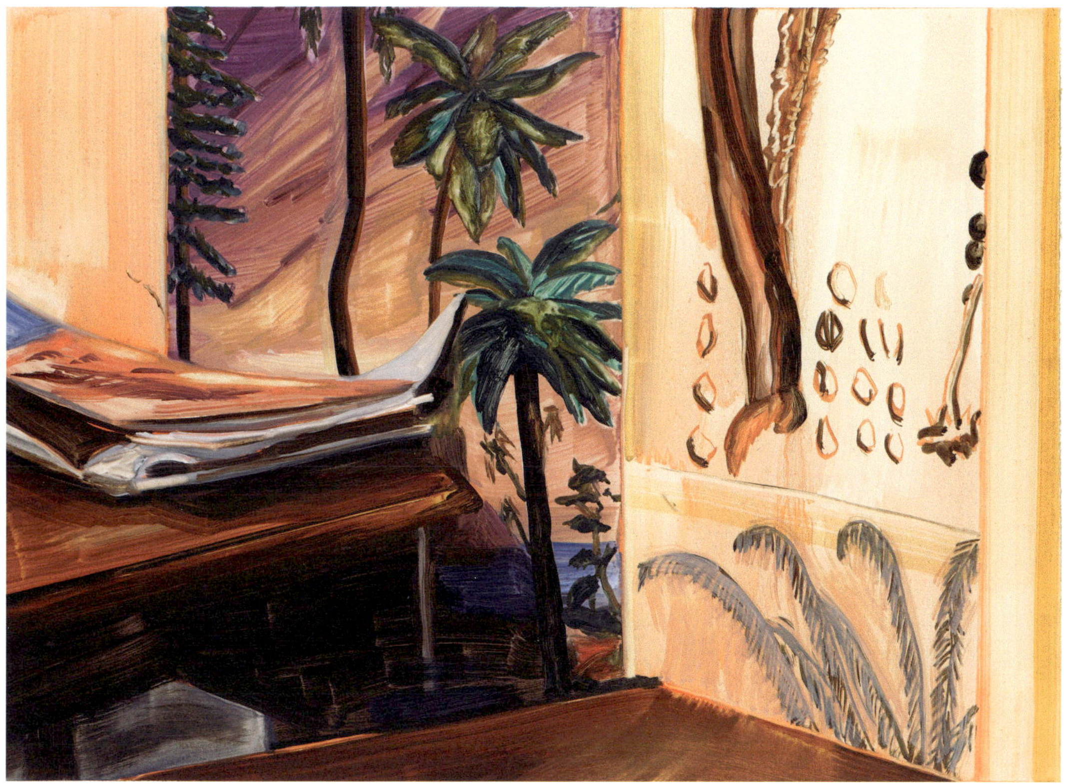

utopian – it is sometimes dystopian, other times heterotopian. Indeed, Freeman Bentley's paintings take us into some kind of heterotopia – into in-between spaces, transitional spaces, uncertain spaces, multivalent spaces. These are places where meaning is accrued, where purpose can be changed by the people using them or the things within them. Amid the densely charged, ever-changing palimpsest of major cites today, through her painting, Freeman Bentley invites us – challenges us, perhaps – to engage with the built environment with our hearts, eyes and minds wide open.

Study for Uproot and Leave, 2014, oil on paper, 34.5 × 49 cm

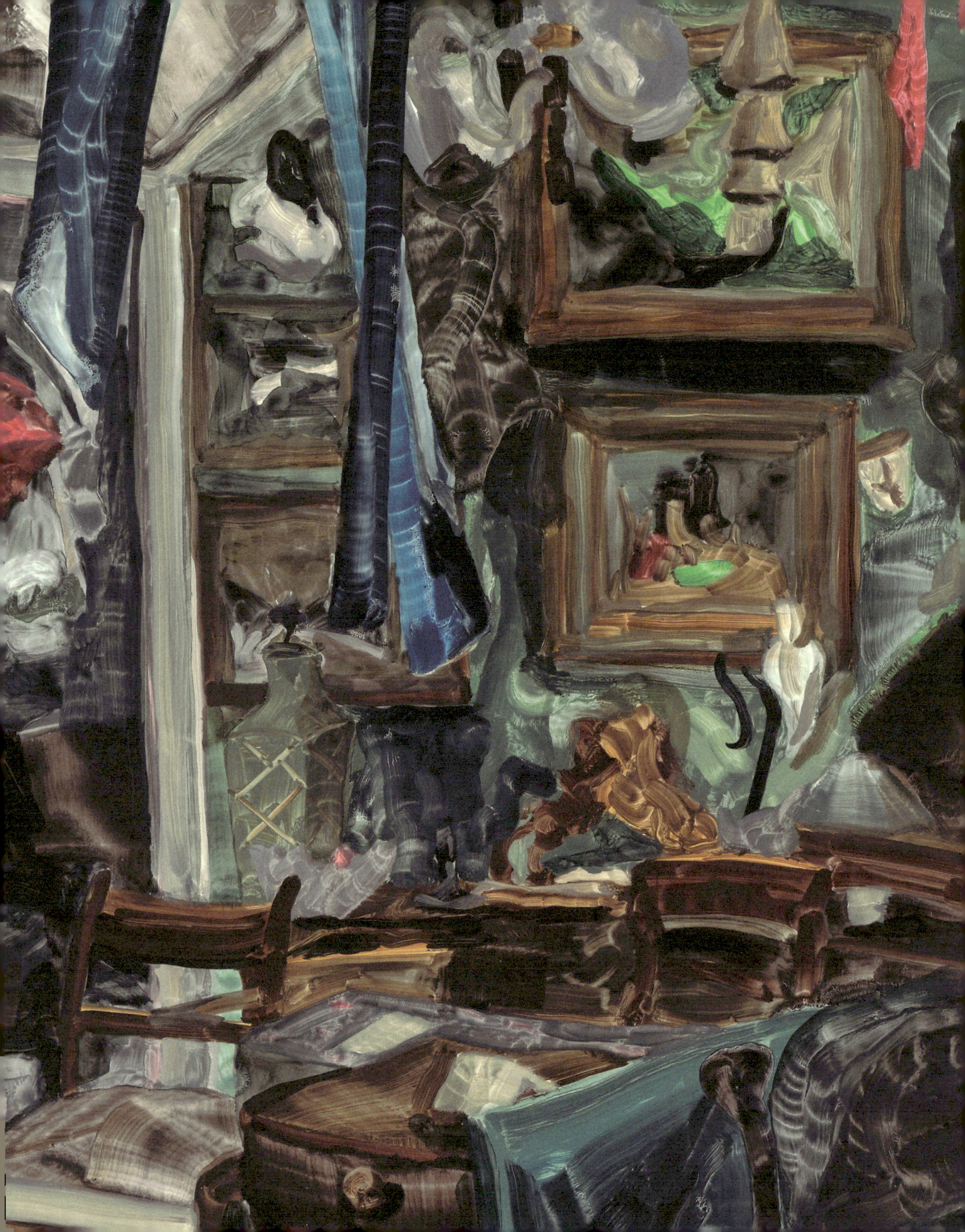

MARINA CASHDAN

Her World of Interiors

In an industrial building in London's Hackney Wick, up the steps, past pigment-spattered slop sinks and through a narrow door, is the studio of painter Anna Freeman Bentley – tidied for my visit, and bright, with oil paints lining the shelves, glass bottles of turpentine along a drawing table which faces two full-height factory windows, and reference photographs tacked up on the adjacent wall. Paintings, small- and large-scale, are hung or carefully leant up against the walls. Other large-scale paintings are coddled in protective packaging beside the door, to or from shipment. The space is unbelievably quiet – none of the industrial sounds one might expect in such a building. Instead, the birds are chirping. The environment feels like a fitting place for the artist to make her work – bright yet constricted, tactile yet sterile, sensual yet sobering. Her studio and its facing view – an industrial landscape that has been transformed into live-work artist spaces and luxury apartments – complement the scenes depicted in her paintings; interiors and architecture that are both desolate and full, human-less and inhabited, apathetic and soulful, free and restrained, and the tension and longing that resound in the space between these dichotomies.

Freeman Bentley was born in London but spent the early part of her life in Thailand and Hong Kong, where her father, a civil engineer, was consulting on the construction of bridges. A common occasion in her household was going with her father to building sites: "For family trips we didn't go to many art museums, but rather he would take us – full of his usual enthusiasm – to look at structures and construction sites," she remembers. "So I have many memories of holding weird gadgets – things I had no idea what they were for, but he was excited about them because they were the latest bit of technology for innovating the construction industry." Later, as a boarding student back in England, Freeman Bentley focused on drama, art and literature. "At the time I was as drawn to literature and drama as to art, but I wanted to continue with art because I felt challenged by it in a particular way," she recalls. "It was something into which I could feed all my inquisitiveness from those other fields." Both influences would come to play an integral role in her later painting practice.

She enrolled on a foundation course at Camberwell in London, where she explored 2D and 3D forms, as well as design and fashion. When it came to determining her specialisation, Freeman Bentley recalls her decision process: "I remember [my tutors] asking me if I liked working to a brief. I said that I was much more interested in pursuing an independent line of inquiry, which landed me in the fine art department where I began making paintings. As one tends to during a foundation year, I was exploring lots of different mediums and materials." At the time, she was making pure abstractions, a "broader

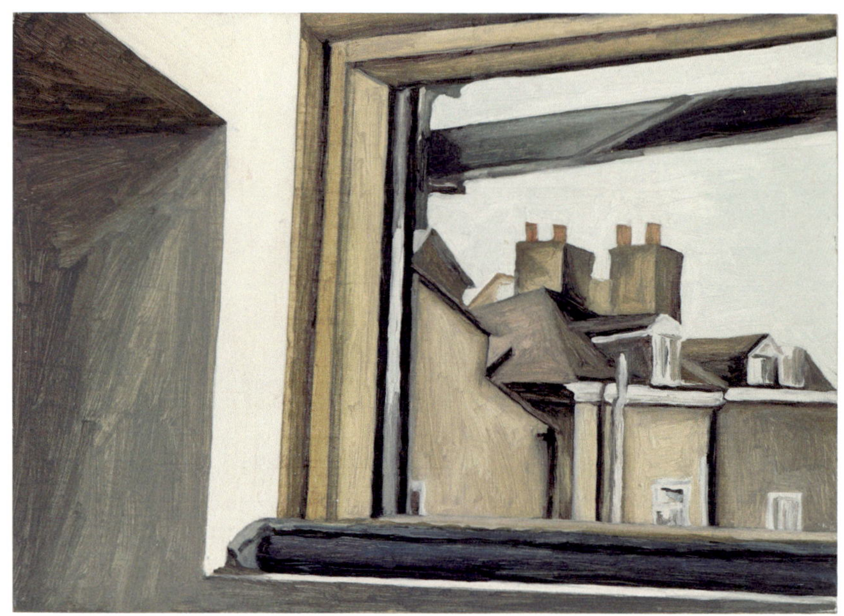

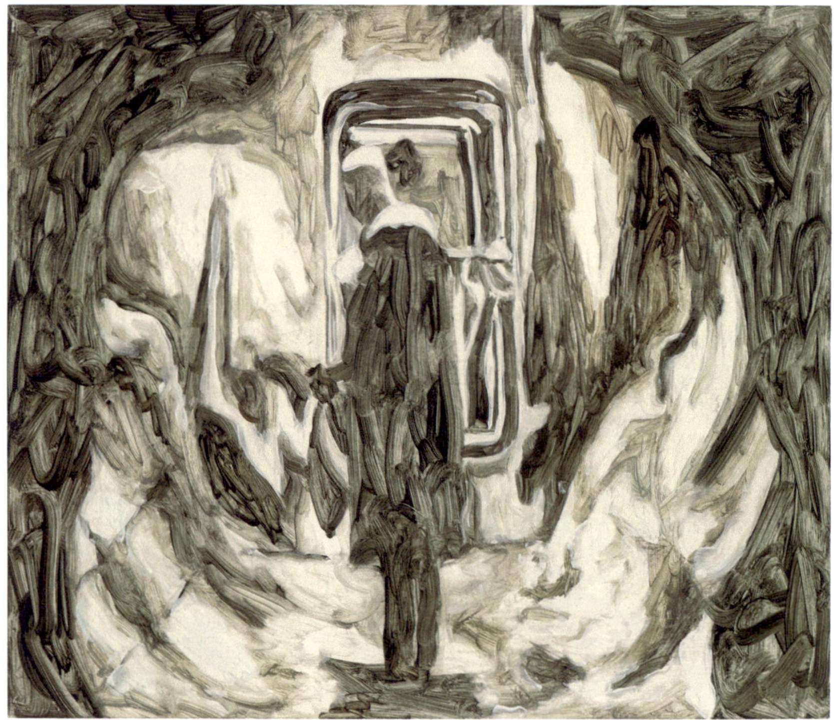

    Looking Out, 2003, oil on board, 12.5 × 17.6 cm   *People Don't Wait Here*, 2004, oil on board, 58 × 69 cm

language" of expression that she felt helped her through the struggle of her father's death only a couple of years earlier. "They almost weren't paintings – they used fabric and collage and varnish; they had bits of cut-out text written in my father's handwriting." Abstract gesture and collage would play a part in her later work.

Though Freeman Bentley was initially intimidated by the history and challenges of painting, one of her tutors, Nick Hacking, encouraged her to apply to painting programmes in London. She was the only student from Camberwell to be accepted on to the painting course at Chelsea College of Art and Design that year. Freeman Bentley started her BA by culling memories from her childhood in Thailand – the smells, the colours, the language, creating further abstracted and textural works. An almost dramatic transition then took place in her second year as she went from abstract to figurative work. And further, her environment in London would lead her to the subject matter she has explored since.

Being in London twelve years ago, there were a lot of abandoned buildings around. I lived in Hackney for much of the time and there were many derelict old factories and warehouses there then. Being inquisitive – and with my research into the atmosphere of a place fresh in my mind from my Thailand series – I just wanted to go in them. So I started exploring these buildings, and found them so powerful – they had this absolute presence of human life and yet they were so empty. I became fascinated by them, so stopped exploring the theme of abstracted Thailand and started making a series of small paintings on cardboard about these structures in London. I put sand on the cardboard so they had a rough texture, then painted more figurative images of the abandoned buildings over the sand, then varnished the paintings.

Freeman Bentley would snap photographs of these abandoned interiors, and her exploration of architecture and interiors would take her first to desolate buildings and then on to attics, theatres, cafes, domestic spaces and junk shops. Starting with her earlier work, Freeman Bentley set clear parameters – the canvases were always human-less and in a muted or colourless palette:

I didn't want to have figures in the spaces because I didn't want to set up a narrative as such. I wanted the projection of the viewer to be into the space rather than onto a figure. The more that I've read about architecture and thought about the work, the more I have become interested in the human nature of spaces without humans in them. I was recently reading in Anthony Vidler's book *The Architectural Uncanny* about architecture in terms of walls that see – walls that gaze out at you. If I were to paint a figure in there, you wouldn't have this sense of being looked at at all, it would become more voyeuristic, more about you looking at the person within the space.

Yet Freeman Bentley leaves traces of human presence – empty chairs, lit candles, open windows.

Working primarily from her own photographs, Freeman Bentley also experimented in using film as subject, which led to a new leap in mark-making. "I made a series of paintings based on Tarkovsky's film *Stalker*. It was a film that had been recommended to me during my first year [at Chelsea], and I kept coming back to it because of how visual it is and of course the connections to the abandoned buildings and the idea of seeking or longing for a space, the room of desire. For my final degree exhibition, I presented a series of works based on film stills from *Stalker*, and that was the only time that I had worked using images that were not my own." [See opposite, below.] The paintings included ghostly figures that evoke the work

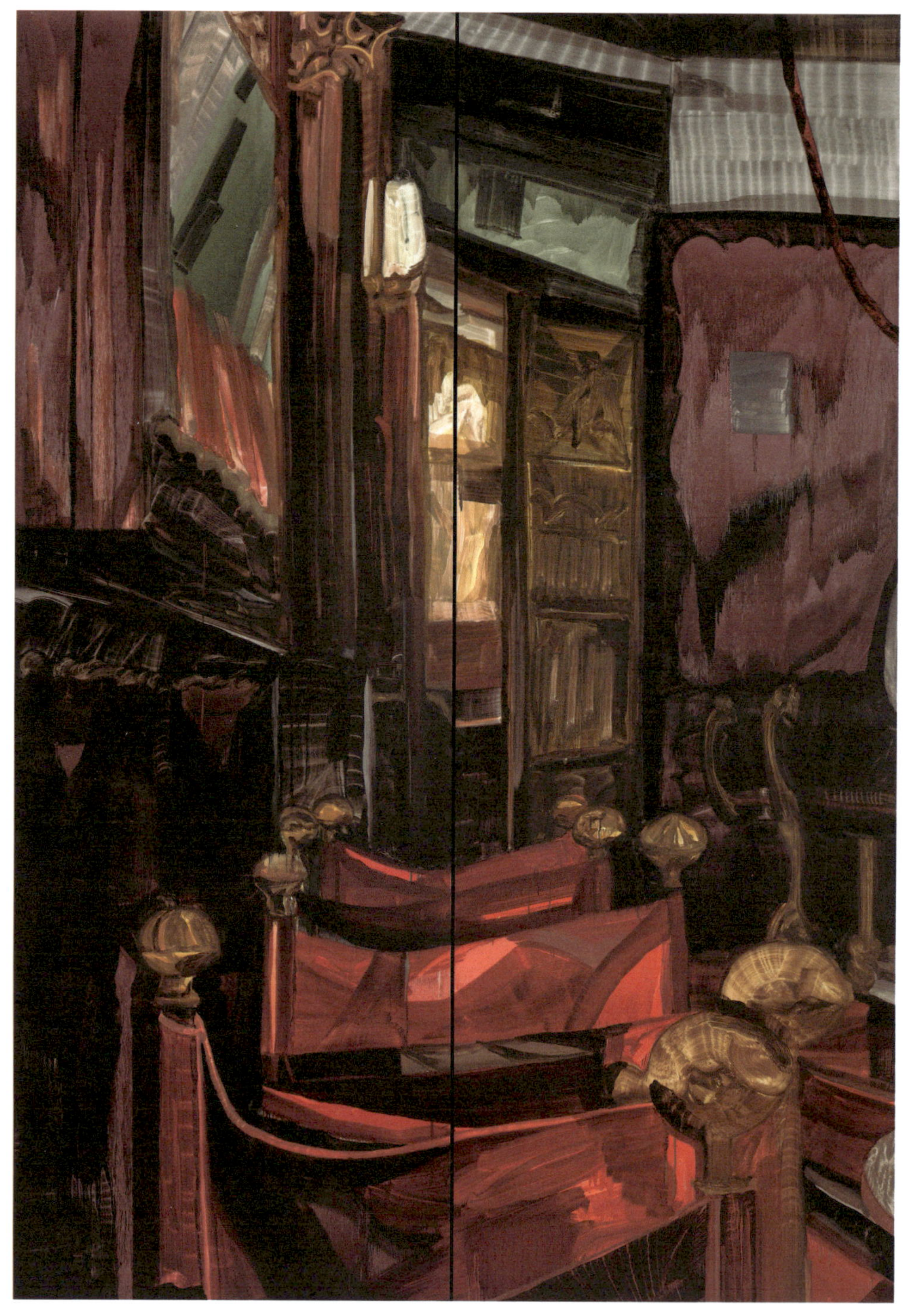

The Approach, 2012, oil on board, 280 × 200 cm (2 panels, 280 × 100 cm each)

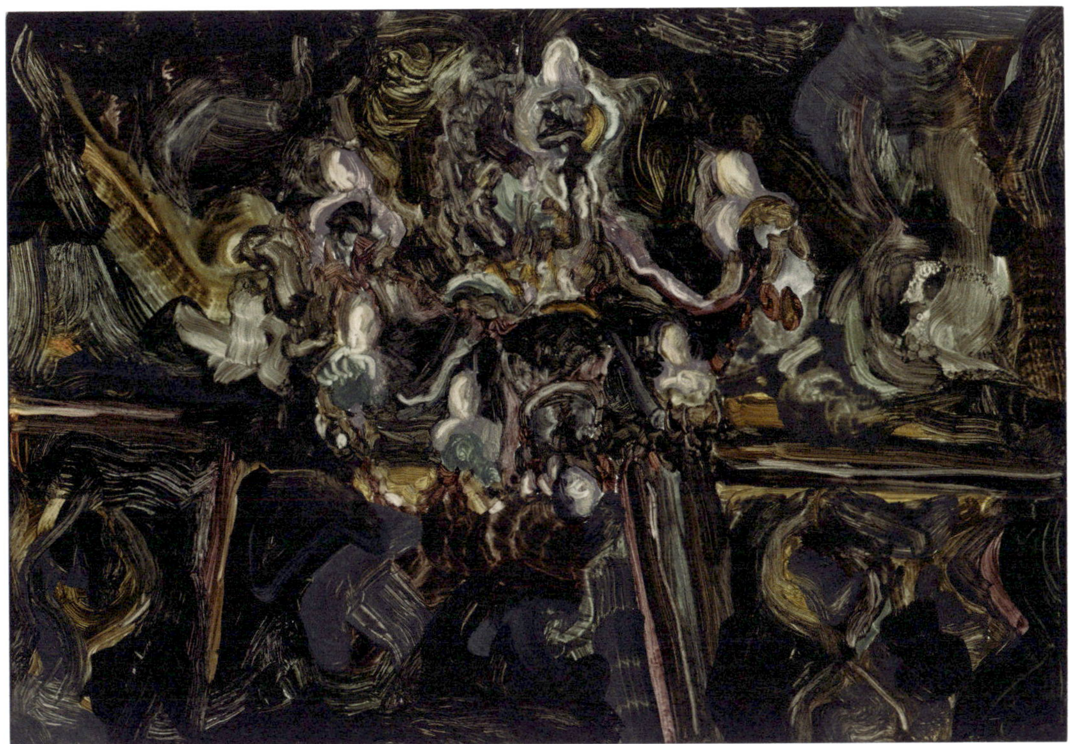

of Luc Tuymans. However, the forms are not painted as figures as such, but rather as objects, or even as elements of the interiors – eliminating any trace of detail in the face or hands, giving the artist the space to make more fluid brushstrokes; this would carry through into her subsequent interior and architectural paintings. Films by directors such as Andrei Tarkovsky, Michelangelo Antonioni and David Lynch would also affect the dynamics that carry through in her work.

During her time at Chelsea College, Freeman Bentley was part of an exchange programme in Berlin, studying at the Kunsthochschule Weissensee under Katarina Grosse. "While I was there I was making work about London, and when I got back to London I was making work about Berlin and all the abandoned buildings I had discovered there (such as the now demolished Palast der Republik). I had thought that making work about somewhere else might be important to my practice because that idea pertained to longing, but whilst that is important, actually I am just interested in notions of place." Notions of place would take her to Venice in 2012 for a solo exhibition which she treated almost as a residency. Here, Venice as a place played the central role in her paintings, representing a shift in her use of paint and application, with forms that appear to be slipping from the canvas, a transience that Freeman Bentley parallels to the city itself, and demonstrated by a work such as *The Approach* (2012) [opposite]. Place, whether literal or spiritual, is a crucial part of Freeman Bentley's process and approach. Her attraction to a place is the starting point for her paintings. She photographs the locations, experimenting

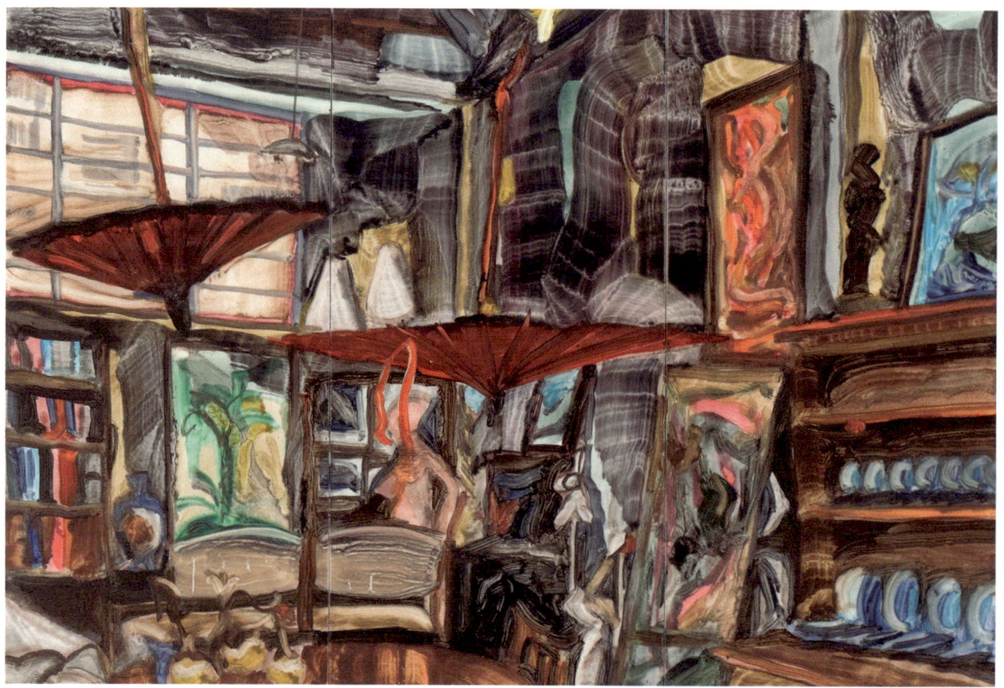

with cropping, framing and composition. And then from her photographs extracts fragments to paint – often taking these moments out of their context or distorting the angle or positioning on the canvas. This imbues her paintings with a mystery – a feeling that is at once psychologically charged and visually magnetic.

It was when Freeman Bentley started the MA Painting programme at the Royal College of Art that her colour palette would transition from a muted tone to blacks and, further, explode with reds, as exemplified by works such as *A Great Light* (2009) [p.17] and *The People Walking in the Darkness* (2009) [p.52]. This shift, she explains, was due to "deepening [her] research in the Baroque. It was also due to a desire to keep pushing the practice forward. I love dark colours and for a long time they were the recipe for making a painting work for me. I would start a painting and if it wasn't working then I would turn to

more black. But having recognised this as a bit of a formula, I was keen to work against it."

After she left the RCA, in 2010, Freeman Bentley took a year-long studio residency at the Florence Trust, housed in a deconsecrated Victorian church in Highbury. "[The residency] culminates in an exhibition in the church where the studios have been. I spent pretty much the whole year making work about junk shops, making ambitious, big paintings, but when it came to the final exhibition at the Florence Trust, I again wanted to make work that related specifically to the architecture there. So I conceived an idea to make the biggest thing I've ever made." She painted a haunting spiral staircase inspired by one she found when visiting the Musée Gustave Moreau in Paris, the former studio of the French Symbolist painter. "I changed and expanded [the Moreau staircase]. I was interested in this idea of the Moreau museum being both a studio

     Waiting and Hoping, 2011, oil on board, 30 × 45 cm (3 panels, 30 × 15 cm each)

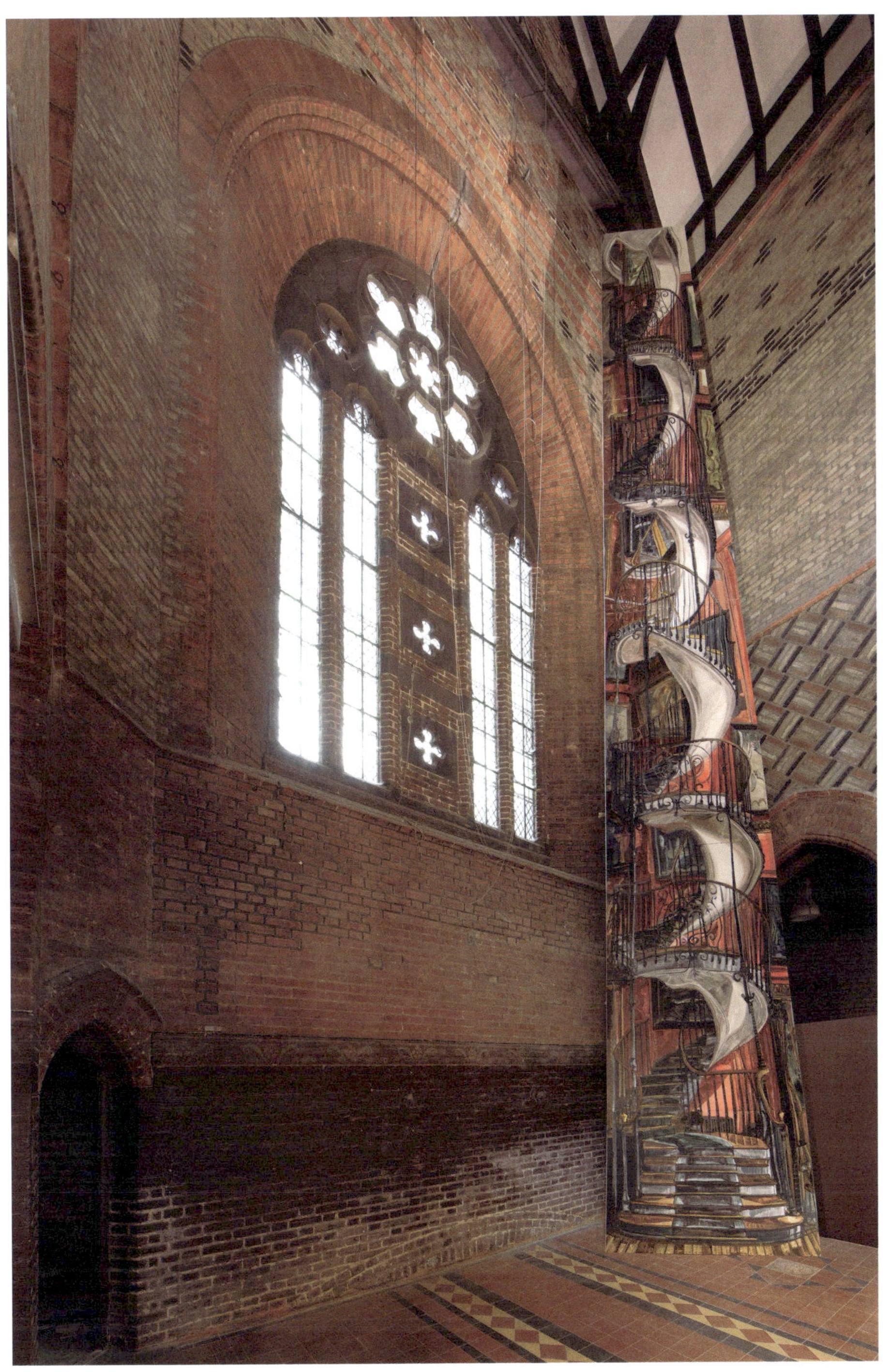

Descent, 2011, oil on 8 panels with tulipwood subframes, 1100 × 182 cm (base) tapering to 91.5 cm (top)

space and an exhibiting space, and that was a connection that I thought would be intriguing, especially as I was about to transform my own studio space at the church into the exhibition space. As soon as I saw the staircase in the museum, I knew the work I wanted to make. It doesn't usually happen like that. It was then just a matter of how to make the idea a reality." [*Descent* (2011) [p.19].]

By installing such a work in a church setting, the artist is also consciously referencing the biblical story of Jacob's Ladder, as suggested in the title of the work, *Descent*, which evokes an image of a staircase reaching down to earth from heaven, a vision that came to Jacob in a dream. Freeman Bentley would recreate that physical and spiritual quality in a 2D and 3D experience, presenting the painting as an architectural installation – eight panels mounted to a scaffolding structure that climbed up the interior of the church. In her MA show at the RCA, Freeman Bentley had begun to explore the notion of painting as installation, mounting two long thin panels to meet at the corner of the gallery. Then on boards of the same size opposing the paintings, she projected a 16mm film of the buildings from which she captured the images. It is works like these that show the artist's interest and historical connection with engineering. Her father was the third generation of civil engineers in his family, with his father and grandfather both being knighted for services to the industry. Freeman Bentley's great-grandfather, Sir Ralph Freeman's most notable achievement was designing the Sydney Harbour Bridge. This is the mind of an engineer's daughter at work, as she combines her visual enquiries with a natural intuition for installing work within structures.

In 2012, Freeman Bentley was invited to be the artist-in-residence at Michelin-starred restaurant Pied à Terre in London.

I was invited to apply for this award, which had a prize of £10,000, a residency and an exhibition. I went to visit the restaurant and was intrigued because it was not somewhere I would have naturally thought of approaching as a space in which to present my work. I spoke to the person who nominated me [Paul Bayley from the Florence Trust] and asked him why he'd nominated me. He said he wanted to see what happened when I was pushed out of my comfort zone. So I went back and thought about it a lot, knowing that the challenge would be good for me. Before that I had been painting a series of junk shop interiors where it was the visual drama of the space that first caught my attention, and I was making work in response to that. But at Pied à Terre, I began to see that it was a space imbued with a drama of its own – a different sort of drama, onc that is not necessarily seen but instead experienced. So naturally I was really excited about working with the space and the team at the restaurant.

She went to the Fitzrovia restaurant once a week to spend time in the kitchens, observing the work of the head chef, Marcus Eaves, and the restaurateur David Moore. She wanted to understand "the ins and outs of what it means to run a restaurant." She also shadowed the waiting staff, the sommeliers and the admin team in the back office. "What I found fascinating about the space was that change of atmosphere when the customers are there compared to when they are not. For me it became like a theatre, and at different times throughout the residency I was involved behind the scenes as well as during the performance."

Freeman Bentley would take this theatrical element and play to it, creating a visually striking theatre in the round, with her work acting as the backdrop to the star of the show: the food. The result was a six-metre-long painting comprising twenty-five narrow, unmounted panels that, together, beautifully accentuated the curved wall

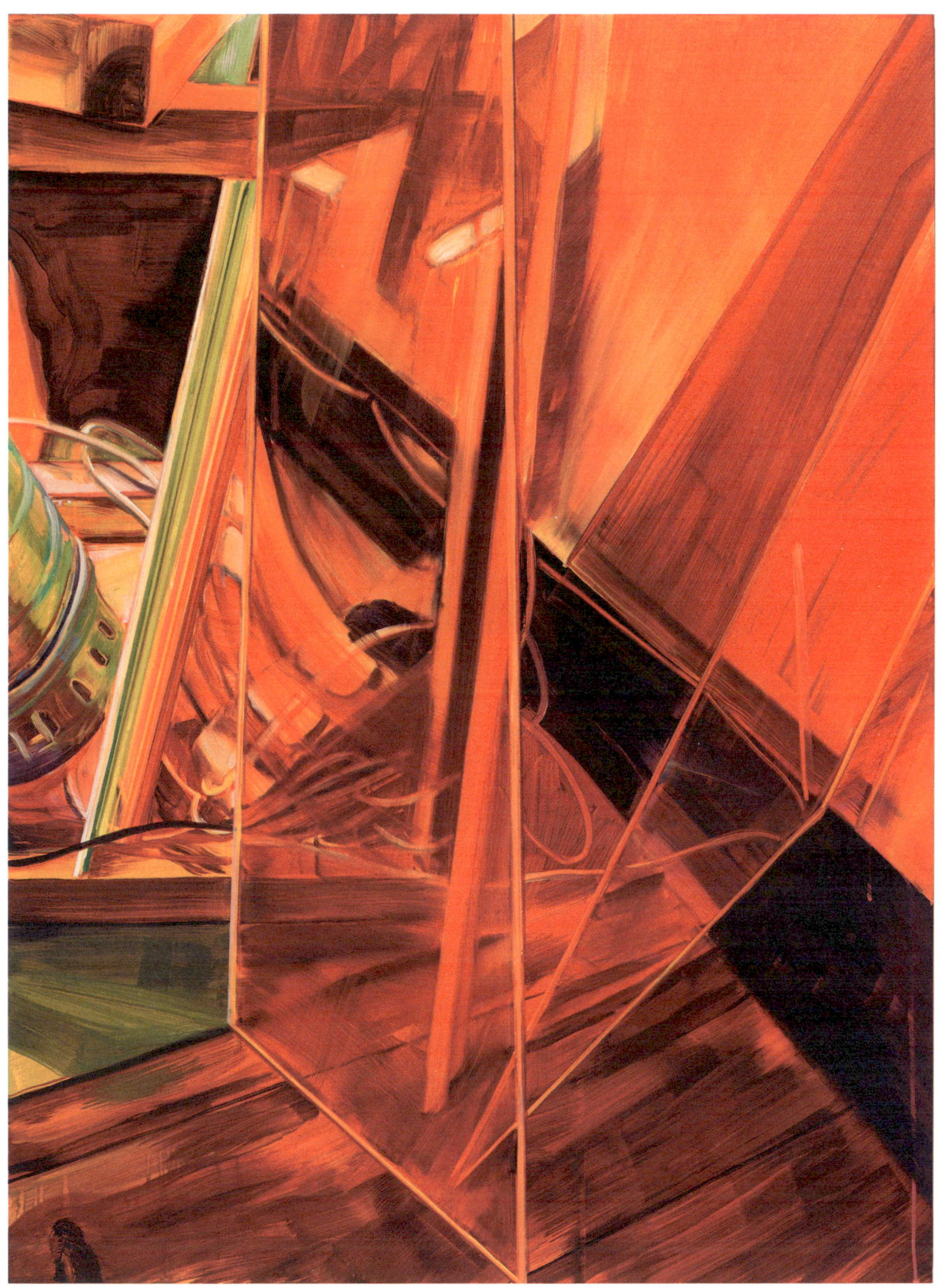

Revival, 2014, oil on board, 120 × 90 cm

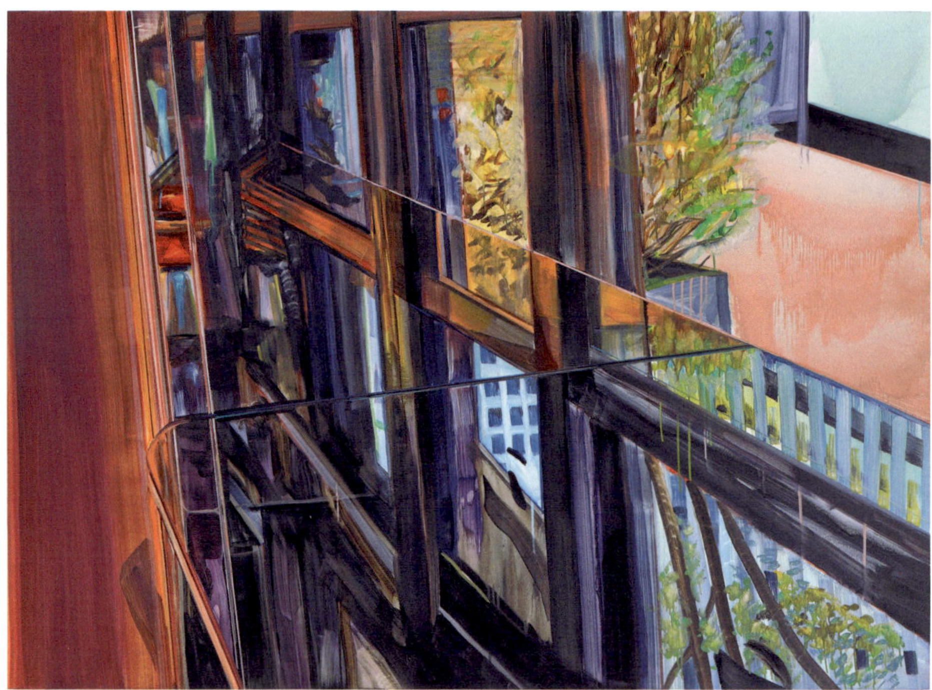

of the dining room. Opposite the installation, a large mirror would reflect the painting back to the viewer and make the work encompass the entire dining area. Mirrors and reflection are a common motif in many of Freeman Bentley's paintings. Depictions of reflected space connect to Foucault's idea of heterotopias as well as to a biblical idea of our present visual experience being only a dim reflection as in a mirror. She had theatrical festoon curtains custom made, and hung them above the mirror to accentuate this theme [see pp.24-6]. And even her colour palette was altered to reflect the intensity of dramaturgy, drawing in cooler colours as a striking counterpart to the deep reds of the baroque pieces she had been working on previously.

Over the past two years, Freeman Bentley has been exploring her interest in collage [see pp.94-7], which has in turn imbued her work with a newfound use of abstraction – geometric splices and dizzying angles become the marriage between the figurative and the abstract, as the watery paint – and the visible drips (a technique Freeman Bentley first started to experiment with in her Venice paintings) – depict candles and the corners of tables, ornate mirrors, mirrored walls, light fixtures, mouldings and bric-a-brac. Progressively the work has also allowed for more colour – the blacks and reds making way for moments of aqua greens, yellows and burnt oranges, demonstrated by a work such as *Revival* (2014) [p.21]. And similarly, the soulfulness of the work becomes more exposed. Freeman Bentley is allowing the vulnerable side to show through. Though she considers the various shifts she has undergone dramatic, to the eye they follow an organic evolution of her practice – an exploration in the finite and infinite, the known and unknown, the understood and otherness.

Orientation, 2014, oil on board, 121 × 170 cm

Collage has always been quite a useful way for me to start approaching images, because I can play around with so many possibilities of space. The work can become a lot more abstract. This year I started working with the abstraction that was already there, in the details of gentrified space. In my own head I always see these transitions as clear breaks, but then someone else will say to me that they can see the follow-through. Even in my BA when I shifted from the abstract work to making the small paintings of abandoned buildings, I felt that it was a really new direction, but my friend pointed out that, in a more subtle way, it was still about my dad. I hadn't seen that at all. While I don't believe this is the primary concern of my work, I acknowledge that it is present, and I do often wonder what kind of conversations I would have had with him about the ideas in my practice, because he was inspired by function and making things work, whereas my work is always driven by the visual, and my memories are very visual. I'm far less interested in how things will operate and much more in how they will look.

Freeman Bentley's current body of work comes full circle, from derelict buildings in East London to, now, the gentrification and renewal of that same area of the city. Some paintings depict refracted scenes of glass-and-steel modern buildings in a palette of blues and greens, evident in a work such as *Orientation* (2014) [opposite], while others show details of wallpaper images in hues of orange and purple, or people-less cafes with leftover newspapers and coffee cups, the sun pouring through shards of neon Perspex, or greenery creeping out from window boxes. Analogously, Freeman Bentley has had a renewal in her own process: "I made a very conscious decision to try to slow down the making of the final product. I spent three months only making works on paper," she says. "I used to only see them as preliminary works, acting as just a step further away from the photograph. [...] But with the decision to slow down [...] I have been making so many works on paper that they've started to elevate themselves in my mind to works in their own right." And so they should – the small-scale oil sketches on paper offer an even more soulful and intimate glimpse into her own interior space and allow her the freedom to be more experimental in subject, palette and application.

A staircase, the abandoned and then found items in a junk shop, the transience of Venice, the hope and despair of abandoned buildings, the rise and fall of Baroque architecture, displacement, regeneration and renewal in a changing urban landscape. In Freeman Bentley's works, an empty space is filled with emotion, memories, conversation and spiritual longing that is at once personal and universal – offering permanence and growth in a world that often shows signs of dissolution.

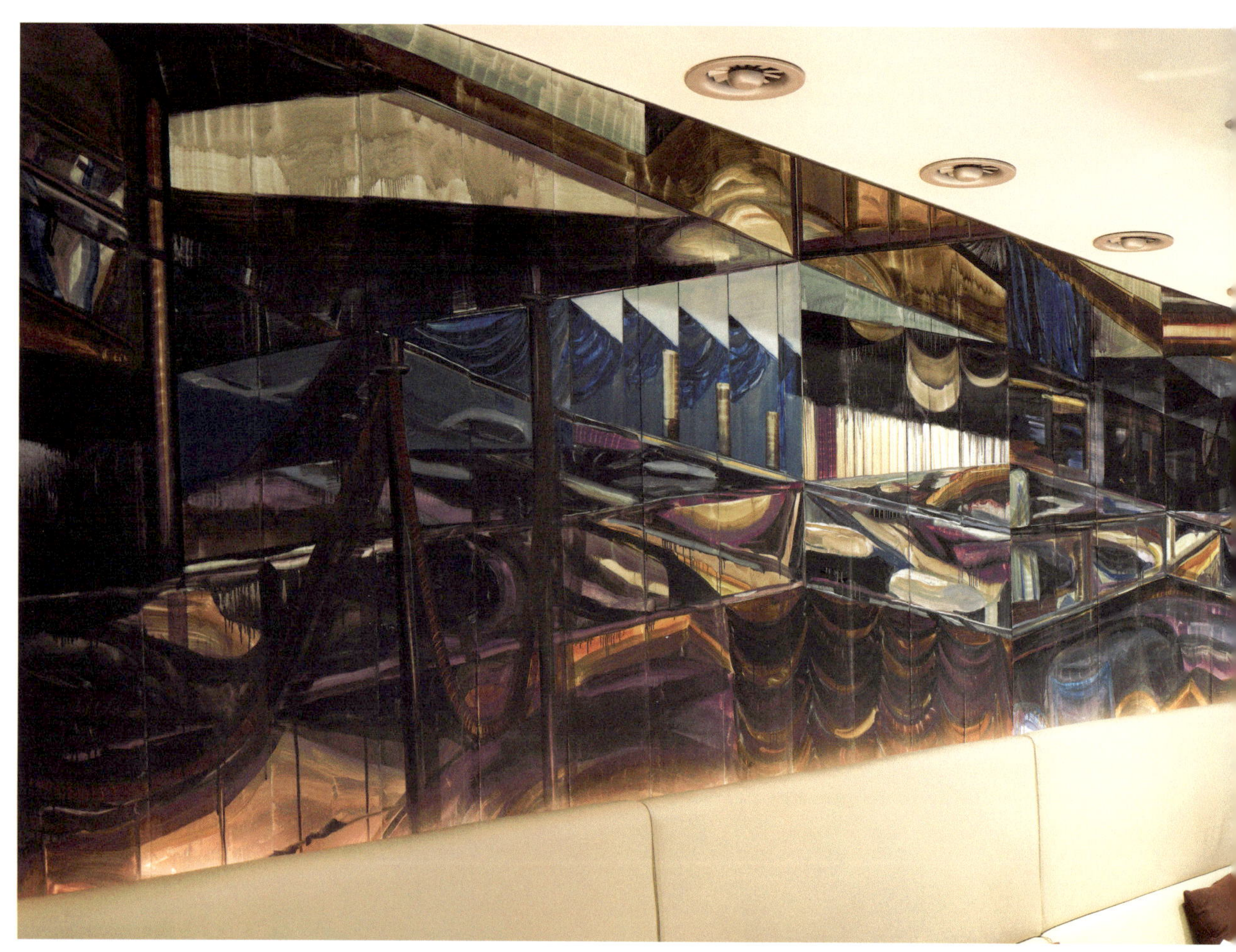

 Restoration, solo exhibition, Pied à Terre, London, October 2012

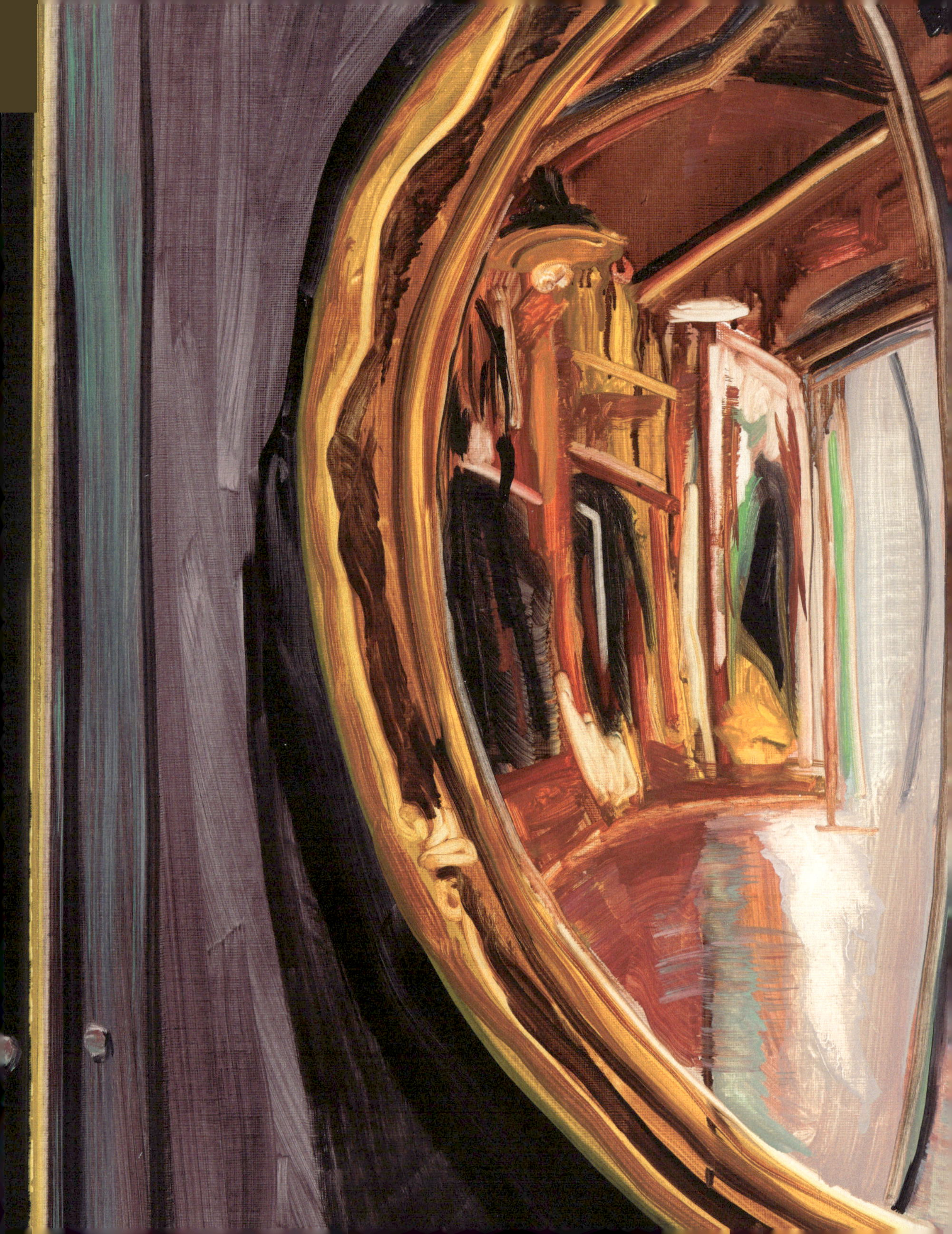

Through a Glass Darkly

Geographies of the Soul

> Because creation is grace, grace is concrete:
> it meets us in […] "the bulks of ordinary
> things" – and this of course includes build-
> ings and settlements, the places in which
> we live and work. The theology of everyday
> life, therefore, is a theology of grace as a
> theology of gratuity, of love "for nothing",
> and of joy in the minutiae of things.[1]

These are words by the contemporary
Christian theologian Timothy Gorringe. Quite
inadvertently, they explain something of the
focus and energy of Anna Freeman Bentley's
work. She is gripped and fascinated by her material environment, by the "bulks" as well as the
"minutiae" of things; and this material environment, with its panoply of buildings and objects,
is for her never just dead matter. There is *spirit*
in the matter. For Freeman Bentley, too, "grace
is concrete", and the everyday environment is
charged with unpredictable possibilities, which
activate deep human longings and hopes.

Despite the fact that the spaces (almost
always interiors) that the artist shows us are
without occupants, they are nevertheless
highly "populated" spaces in that they are
full of human concern and life. To borrow a
term coined in the 1950s, these spaces offer us
psychogeographies. Packed with objects that
people once manufactured but that may now

have lost their original context, and offering
unbidden viewpoints across uncertain distances,
her images take us off our customary paths. The
world of well-ordered utility (where everything is
"for something", and it is clear exactly what that
something is in every case) is shown to be more
fluid and less stable than we generally suppose.
Physical matter constantly drifts (as do we).
But in losing their connection with what they
were originally for, Freeman Bentley's interiors
and objects enact an openness to gratuity – to
sometimes being (gratuitously) for nothing
rather than (purposively) for something.

As such, they become messengers of a
sort of excess. Not the excess of mere quan-
tity, manifest in the heaps of unnecessary or
no-longer-needed physical material with which
we surround ourselves. This is an excess of a very
different kind: an excess of *possibility*, in which
(to use Jacques Maritain's words) things can be
"more than they are", and "give more than they
have", because they are shown to have a dignity
and a destiny beyond their merely utilitarian
(human) uses.[2] In turn, this dignity and destiny
beyond mere use (this gratuity) can be seen as
analogous to what theology calls *grace*: a regen-
erative power permeating all things. Grace is
the excessive, gratuitous gift of an uncompelled
divine love at work in the world; a love for things
not because of what they can give back to their
creator (who lacks nothing), but simply for their
own sakes. Such excess harbours redemptive

possibilities for the places, things and people in which it discloses itself.

In light of this it can be argued that while Freeman Bentley's works are sometimes emotionally powerful, they are also *spiritually* powerful. In raising questions about loss, grace and possible redemption, she is exploring something deeper than human emotion. Emotionally, the traces of memory and association she explores in her dislocated spaces awaken feelings such as nostalgia, disillusionment, desire, fear and envy. But there are deeper dynamics in the atmosphere: qualities beyond what we ourselves bring to these spaces; other energies that are at work, suggesting that their small histories might be part of a bigger history, and that as made things these objects and places might have original depths and future ends that (mirroring our own) are not merely finite but also eternal, and as such not yet seeable. The unseen is traced in the dislocated seen.

You might say that the artist offers us psychogeographies of a very particular sort; almost certainly not those that a 1950s Situationist manifesto would have had in mind. The Situationist International transformed the idle drifting of the flâneur, whose search was for transient stimuli to combat boredom, into a definite political programme; Freeman Bentley transforms it into the spiritual openness of the religious seer; of the believer. Both activist and seer need to be ready for surprise, for revelations of the unexpected, but while the Situationist aimed to discover a level of authentic feeling that would act as a remedy for advanced capitalism's fetishism of the object, Freeman Bentley enacts a sort of prophetic searching into what lies beyond the familiar appearances of things, and into how (once they have been prised free of our ordering and appropriative grasp) both things and places can be given back to us as more than we guessed they could be. The "psyche" in Freeman Bentley's psychogeography carries its earlier theological and original Greek meaning of "soul" or "spirit". She is in search of how we, as material creatures, are on a journey through physical matter towards death, and how those of faith understand themselves as being on pilgrimage towards an abiding home to which even death does not put an end.

This is because she is an artist whose practice is profoundly influenced by her own Christian faith. An awareness of Christian themes and theological ideas helps an understanding of her work, and her work in turn opens a set of dialogues with a tradition of religious thought that is too often ignored by contemporary art criticism. As a theologian I find her work richly suggestive.

Crop Rotation

> [The modern city is] the lightning rod of the profoundest human discontents, and the arena of social and political conflict. It is a place of mystery, the site of the unexpected, full of agitations and ferments, of multiple liberties, opportunities and alienations; of passions and repressions; of cosmopolitanism and extreme parochialisms; of violence, innovation and reaction.[3]

If Anna Freeman Bentley's work is readable as a form of theology, then one of the most obvious things it reflects upon theologically is urban life. But the city is an ambiguous place in Christian tradition. "The city originates in the refusal of Eden, humankind's provided home, and the substitution of a home [that] humankind provides for itself."[4] Both Cain and Nimrod – violent men – are said in Scripture to have been the founders of cities. And yet, in the Book of Revelation, the city is also "the model of what will finally be redeemed, the paradigm of the human home and the focus of human creativity."[5] Cities are recognised as being capable of generative spiritual lives. They have a place in the economy

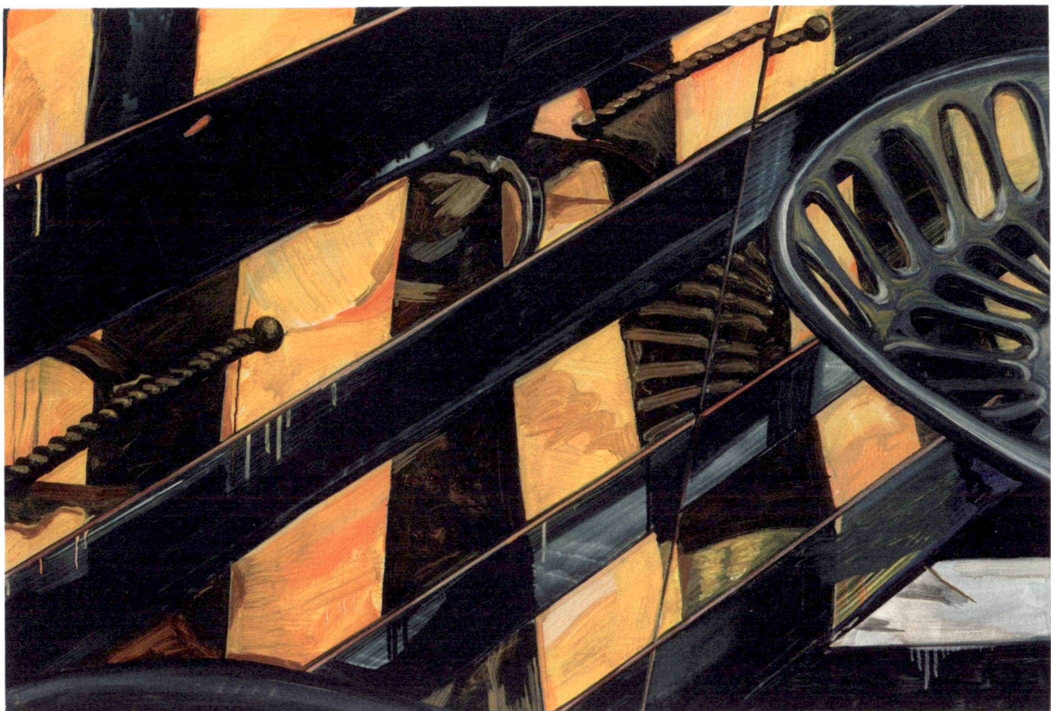

of redemption, and the Christian Bible ends with the vision of a redeemed city.

This very urban tension between violence and redemption is at the heart of much of Freeman Bentley's work – and also of her method. With an acknowledged fascination for cinematic techniques, which crop and rotate images to stimulate interrogation and open us to surprise, she makes decisions to cut things out, push parts of her objects outside the frame, refuse some angles in favour of others. These cropping techniques have a nearly violent quality about them, inasmuch as cutting is an act of forceful exclusion as well as of straitened inclusion. And such violent connotations will also be recognisable to those who have experienced the urban dynamics of displacement and replacement that are a feature of modern cities – cities marked by increasingly rapid changes to earlier, more settled patterns of ownership, and by the conflicts that arise when culturally different groups are thrown together in a small space.

More specifically, by enacting cropping and rotating processes in her work, we might say that Freeman Bentley enacts an artistic parallel to the processes of displacement and renewal that go with gentrification.

The displacement of one order by another, newer order is often a disturbing dynamic; historically speaking, entering a Promised Land has usually entailed evicting (or worse) someone else. It involves battles. And the Promised Lands held out to those buying and doing up houses today in areas of post-industrial cities where lower income groups previously lived entail casualties of their own. In processes of gentrification, a population that has lived in and enjoyed a place finds itself, often forcibly, displaced from it. Landlords and developers move in, social housing becomes private housing, and property prices rise. There is a rotation of habitation; a change. As Hedley Smyth has argued, and Gorringe highlights, this is a process "already well evidenced in London". The displacement of lower income groups as a result of "urban renewal and gentrification" means that "many will come to live in a transition zone" as a consequence.[6]

Many of Freeman Bentley's recent works take stock of these processes. The euphemisms of regeneration that are used to reconcile us to such processes often disguise the fact that they are indeed a sort of cropping. Buildings are cut down, and people are cut out. What may be a liberation when viewed from some angles introduces a new set of exclusions when approached from others. An "old geezers' pub" in Hackney that is transformed into a trendy bar will rarely see an old geezer cross its threshold again – nor, for that matter, welcome a farmer onto its adapted tractor seats (see *Trace* (2014) [p.31] or *Remains* (2014) [p.87]). Indeed – whether on grounds of gender, or spending power or vocation – the artist herself may feel alienated from this environment both in its former and in its latter incarnations.

Nevertheless, in a number of her recent works Freeman Bentley does enter such spaces, to observe these transition zones: their change from one condition to another. Her paintings show us warehouses, junk shops, old factories, as well as new luxury flats, and defunct shops that are now bars and cafes. By meditating on them, she stakes a sort of claim to them – a right to be there too, and to question some of the other methods by which possession or access is secured.

And in doing so, she shows that there can also be generative consequences to these sometimes aggressive changes. To echo David Harvey in the quotation with which this section began, where there is violence there is often innovation as well, just as in visual terms to crop and rotate a viewpoint is to make room for new insight. The violence of displacement and rotation that cities undergo has the power to release new energies and new making at the same time. Where there is no change – no cropping, no rotation – there is death. "[C]reative cities," writes Gorringe, "are places in which social relationships, values and views of the world are in the throes of transformation."[7] He goes on to quote Peter Hall in a similar vein: "Probably no city has ever been creative without continual renewal of the creative bloodstream."[8]

> Conservative, stable societies will not prove creative; but neither will societies in which all order, all points of reference, have disappeared. To a remarkable degree, creative cities have been those in which an old established order, a too-long established order, was being challenged or had just been overthrown.[9]

Anna Freeman Bentley is alert to her own implication in the ethically complex and compromising processes she observes, for, as is widely remarked, art often rides in the vanguard of gentrification. When artists move to a place, money frequently follows; new shifts in social relations are set in train; and finally, after the "in-between time" of artistic presence, the artists move on – priced out of a place by a process to which they contributed. Acutely aware of what it is to be caught up in such processes of transition, Freeman Bentley shows a compassion in these works: she is sympathetic to as well as critical of those who are cropped and those whom rotation brings.

Style and Substance

So Anna Freeman Bentley is, in part, a social commentator through her practice. But, as we

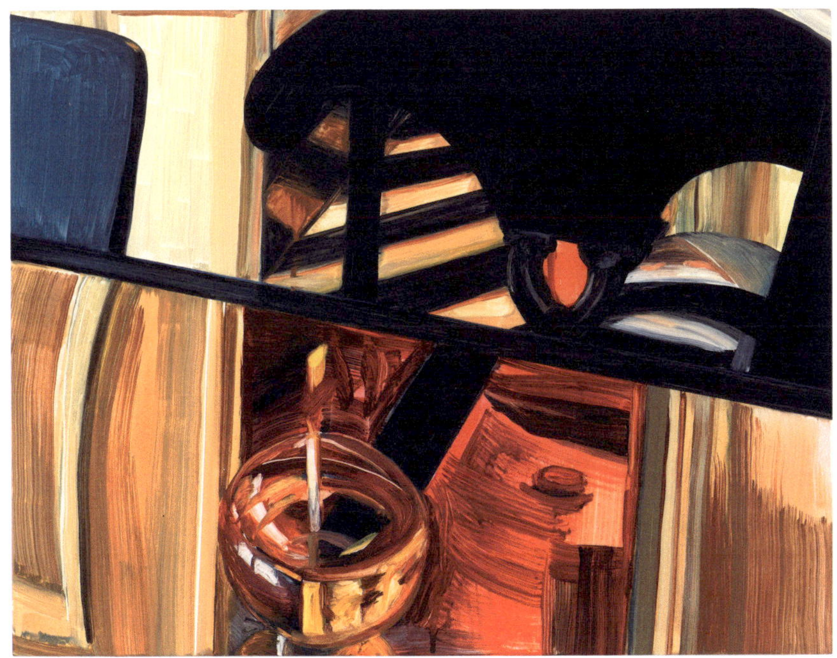

have already hinted, her work is readable at
more than one level. Yes, her paintings are a
form of social commentary: their techniques and
their content are a meditation on ambiguous
experiences of transience and processes of
change, which can be deeply poignant, and often
have victims, while also incubating fascinating
new contexts for human life. But these urban
processes can in turn be read as significant signs
or traces of something more comprehensively
(spiritually) true of the human condition,
which is that the created world itself is in deep
transition. Thus, and to recall an earlier point,
the artist questions the "fors" which we deploy
as a bulwark against the unknown, and does so
in the most fundamental way. To show how the
"for" of things can change at a social (or even a
basic material) level is at the same time to raise
a provocative question about what *anything* (or
everything) is for. What (or who) are *we* for? Are
we even, ultimately, the ones who decide?

In Christian theological terms, spirit (and
more specifically, the Holy Spirit) repurposes
material things, and also the social contexts in
which they are put to use, directing them towards an ultimate and eschatological end. Water,
for example, is changed from "mere" water
– to be used for drinking or washing – and is
consecrated as a medium for personal regeneration and spiritual renewal when it is used as the
material medium of baptism. It acquires a new
power of meaning in this new context; a power
to point from the seen to the unseen, and from
the transient present to the eternal future.

Freeman Bentley plays constantly with
context in her work, making us ask about our
dependency on contexts for the interpretation
and valuing of the objects we find within those
contexts. Often she will use compositional
devices such as mirrors, reflections and close-
ups to disrupt a given perspective in order
to see what sort of new evaluations emerge

Estranged, 2014, oil on board, 40 × 52.5 cm

as a consequence. She will show us the edges of objects, surfaces and spaces which only occasionally give us the "whole" thing (as we normally conceive "things"). She seems to ask what makes a thing whole in the end anyway. Might it not be its relations to other things? Its sharing of space with odd bedfellows, as low-cost table decorations take up occupancy of high-spec designer bars in newly gentrified East London (*Spliced* (2014) [p.81] or *Estranged* (2014) [p.33]), or former tractor seats invite the occupancy of urban drinkers (see the aforementioned *Trace* or *Remains*), or old theatre lights illuminate modern shards of neon Perspex to sell vintage designer clothing (see, for example, *Revival* (2014) [p.21] or *An Awakening* (2014) [p.88])? Or might what makes such things whole be their future juxtapositions with other things in contexts that are not yet apparent? There is excitement and energy in her posing of these questions.

Sometimes, and in ways that may exceed her own conscious intention, her visual splicings and graftings offer unexpected possibilities for interpretation: a cruciform shape emerges, for example, as a central feature of *Abide* (2011) [opposite], constituted by the axes of the back of an ornate decorative headboard and a drooping flag; and in this semiotically rich but unpredictable context the word "oil" on a fuel sign is able take on almost sacramental significance, evoking associations of abundance, of anointing, or of healing.

Sensitive to the nuances of aesthetic style (and its relation to lifestyle), the artist asks about the extent to which the value placed on particular contexts is bestowed on them by an elaborate and cosmetically canny styling. By loosening our grasp on the visual locations that she shows us, she unsettles the ways in which highly wrought decor is deployed to serve very targeted ends, often venially commercial ones — this by contrast with other locations, where objects are jumbled together by accident and where outcomes are more intriguingly unpredictable. This is once again to interrogate the relation of seen to unseen things — here, the relation of style (which is always seen) to substance (which may be unseen) — and to suggest how readily style can obscure rather than mediate things of deep value.

In these aspects, Freeman Bentley's is work that explores notions of integrity and ethos. Just as some buildings that were once built with good intent (out of faith or civic pride, or for public service, or in the name of moral or social improvement) can lose their connection with that original vision, so, nevertheless, new connections can be imagined in other locations. She prompts us to think about how urban planning and capital investment may not be the only ways in which areas are improved; how there are other sorts of "substance": good governance, charitable and religious activity, and the solidarities of community. An affluent veneer cannot hide the underlying atmosphere of an area that is no one's real home, and (by contrast) a run-down but well-run place where a loyal clientele associate may be a triumph of substance over style.

And she asks about how such issues may have a more all-encompassing context still, one in which the substance of human life and relationships finds its ultimate fulfillment: a context, which for her and for many Christians, is one of transforming grace — the power of the Holy Spirit to bring about change, to renew or to breathe new life into places, things and people. Again, the idea of an eternal home beyond our ever-shifting settlements and our proneness to decay is raised here. The idea of heaven (the longed-for final resting place of souls which is central to Christian hope) is made present indirectly through its absence: the vision of what is not yet present is conjured by the spectacle of what is now passing away. Our present abodes are cast as the anteroom of a truer abiding-place, a dwelling that is with and in God.

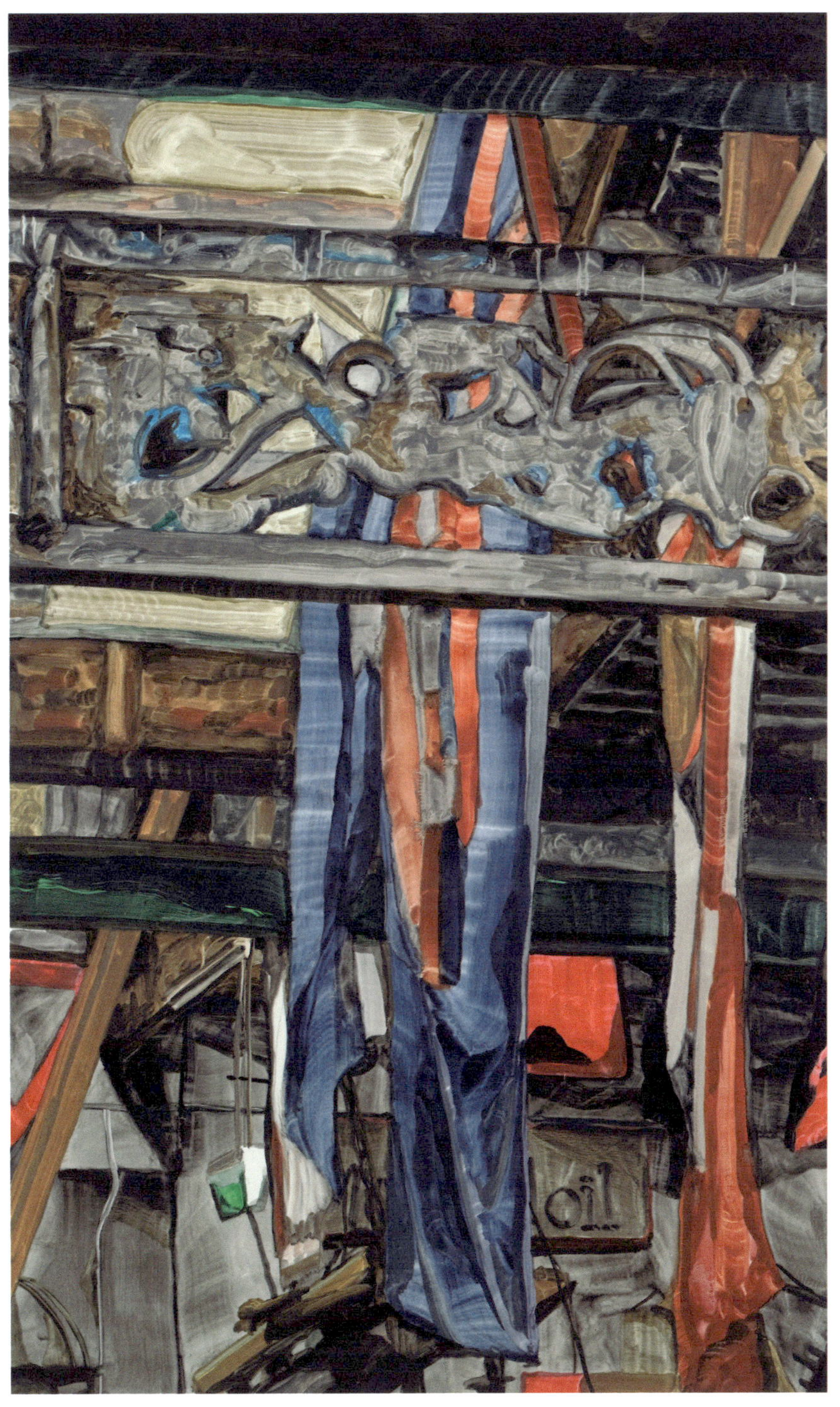

Abide, 2011, oil on board, 200 × 122 cm

But, as the artist believes, this context is not yet fully revealed and for now we see through a glass, darkly.[10]

Loft Living

Anna Freeman Bentley's most recent works have a new vividness of colour, and some more emphatic uses of line than in her previous bodies of work. But in giving a heightened sense of definition, these works paradoxically also heighten the sense of disorientation and uncertainty that has been a consistent preoccupation for the artist. What are we looking at? From what angle? And could we ever enter the spaces that we are being shown?

A popular form of gentrification in recent years has been the loft conversion. As we have noted, urban spaces are very rarely virgin spaces, and the converted loft stands as one of the most common examples of domestic reappropriation and restyling in modern times, whether in the roofs of old houses, industrial buildings such as factories and warehouses, or repurposed period or historic buildings. In many of Freeman Bentley's works, it feels as though we are being taken high up into the rafters – into places that in the past were repositories of half-forgotten objects (and their associated memories), but which seem also to have a peculiar promise. They are old but they are capable of newness; once largely unused but now destined for regular occupation; dark and dingy, now light and bright. Moreover, as high-up places – however enclosed – they have the capacity to offer a vantage point onto multiple worlds below.

Lofts, or attics, have repeatedly accrued associations of mystery, curiosity and adventure. In C.S. Lewis' *The Magician's Nephew*, a prequel to *The Lion, the Witch and the Wardrobe*, his two child protagonists Digory and Polly, lodging in neighbouring houses, begin an adventure by discovering behind the cistern in the attic of one house a passageway along the rafters that connects this house to all the others in the terrace:

> The dark place was like a long tunnel with brick wall on one side and sloping roof on the other. In the roof there were little chinks of light between the slates. There was no floor in this tunnel: you had to step from rafter to rafter, and between them there was only plaster. If you stepped on this you would find yourself falling through the ceiling of the room below. […]
> "Look here," [Digory] said. "How long does this tunnel go on for? I mean, does it stop where your house ends?"
> "No," said Polly. "The walls don't go out to the roof. It goes on. I don't know how far."[11]

By way of this tunnel, and the use of some magic rings, the children are transported to the "Wood between the Worlds": a place that they are helped to interpret by their experience in the rafters. For the Wood between the Worlds is not one place (one world) alongside others, it is a place to which all worlds are connected: a sort of portal to all worlds, just as the passageway in the roof gave access to all the houses.

Freeman Bentley's work goes into spaces that, although mundane and crowded with familiar objects, are also somehow exotic – and the fact that one often cannot see where things end (as in Polly and Digory's tunnel) gives a sense simultaneously of the restriction of one's literal vision, and the awakening of a sense of infinity. Where a property developer's loft conversion might seek to fix a place's possibilities and value by appropriating it as a new piece of real estate, the artist tries to remain in touch with the indeterminacy and openness embodied in its prior use (or neglect). She is not interested in places where people are settled under the illusion of permanent occupancy. Rather, she is interested in places which, because they are unclaimed or unfixed by established usage, also

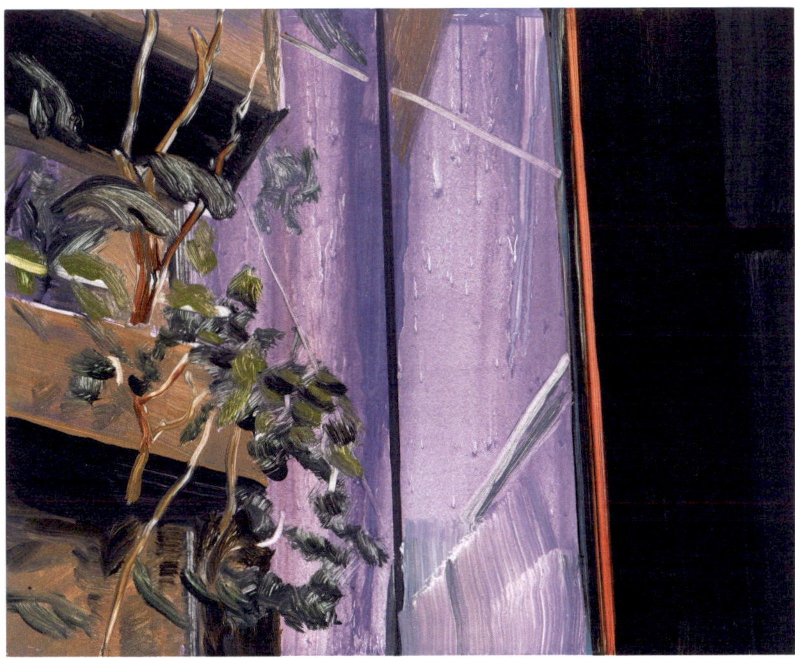

have the power to transport. In many instances they seem uncanny, absurd or surreal. In showing them to us, the viewers of her work, she aims to nudge us towards new experience. As the two late-Victorian children in *The Magician's Nephew* exclaim:

> It's in the houses that people talk, and do things, and have meals. Nothing goes on in the in-between places, behind the walls and above the ceilings and under the floor, or in our own tunnel. But when you come out of our tunnel you may find yourself in any house. I think we can get out of this place into jolly well Anywhere![12]

As Lewis cleverly makes the space in the roof a shadow and premonition of the magical Wood between the Worlds in which there is "a world at the bottom of every pool", so the fluidly shimmering surfaces of Freeman Bentley's

eccentric human spaces (see, for example, *View* (2014) [above] or *Build Up* (2013) [p.75]) seem to be membranes that one might fall through – upwards, downwards or sideways – into something intimated, enticing, but as yet ungraspable. The wallpaper that fascinates the artist in, for example, *Social* (2014) [p.9], *Uproot and Leave* (2014) [p.86], or *Mobility and Grandeur* (2014) [p.93], is made from pages of a book about exotic vegetation, and its plants and trees made the wall of the London cafe into a set of windows onto multiple other locations.

C.S. Lewis' attic space has as part of its literary prehistory the long corridor of doors in which Lewis Carroll's Alice finds herself early in her adventures, the smallest of which gives her a (cropped) glimpse of a garden she cannot initially enter. She then embarks on a series of wild improvisations with her physical size and viewpoint, by drinking a liquid that shrinks her and eating cake that grows her. Here, too, we

View, 2014, oil on board, 15 × 25 cm

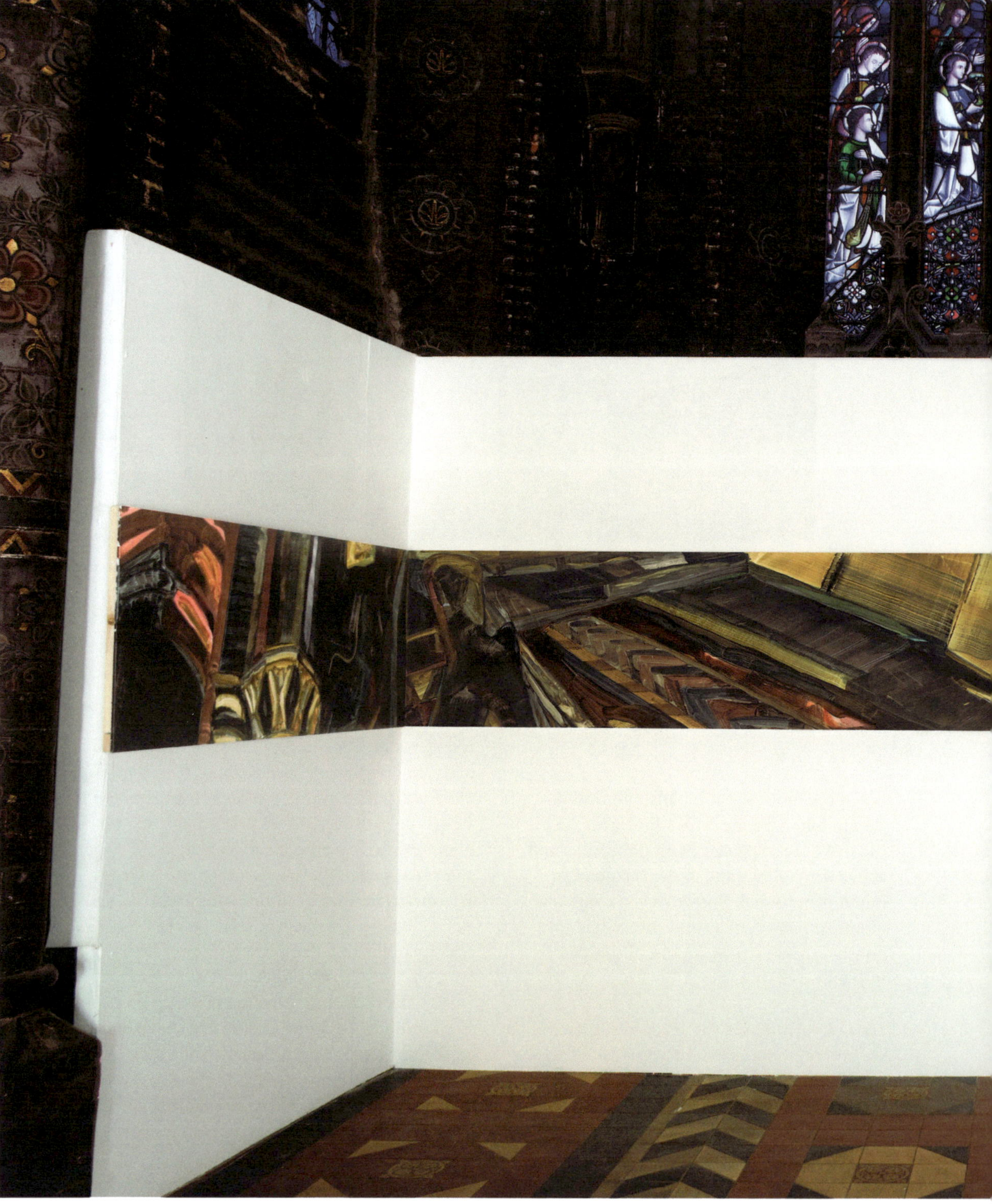

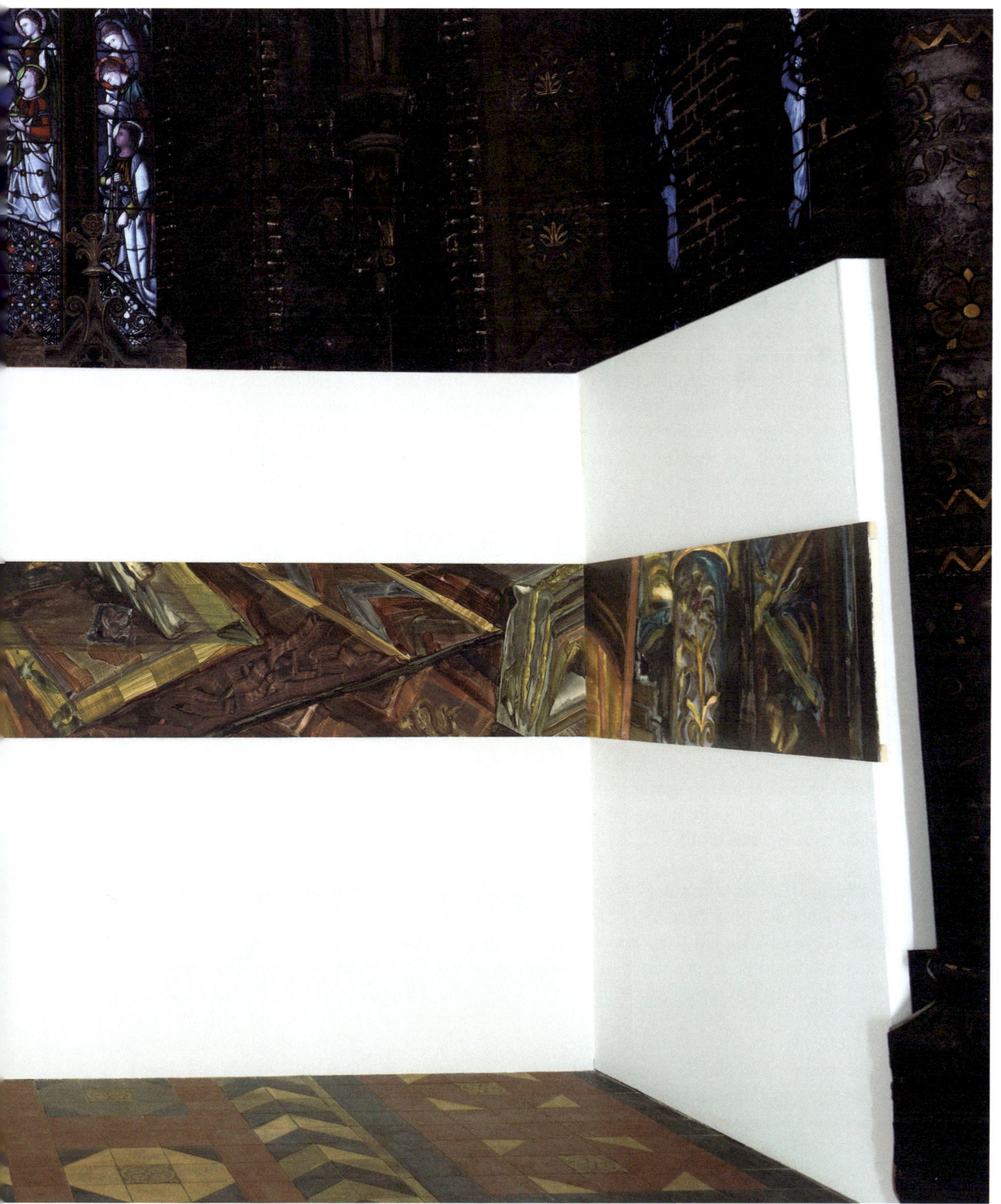

find a parallel to Freeman Bentley's instinct to engage in energetic improvisation with scale and perspective, and her sense of the intrigue, as well as frustrated longing, these experiments can arouse. In the aforementioned *An Awakening*, a series of openings stretches indefinitely away from us, and we are not certain whether we are the right size to fit through them. And often, in both her earlier and later works, we are not sure whether we are seeing a small object from very close, or a great object (a building, for example) from far away – or a mixture of both.

We also wonder whether the spaces we move through are all there is, or whether there is more to be looked for beyond them; whether there are unseen but circumambient dimensions to our reality that might yet be disclosed to us.

Complex Space

Freeman Bentley has been influenced by Michel Foucault's concept of the "heterotopia" – a complex space in which different worlds seem to overlap and interact at once. Foucault holds up the boat as a quintessential heterotopic space in this connection, because it is in itself a contained space, giving the illusion of stability, which is at the same time in constant transition. Its entire circumambient environment shifts all around it constantly, and it is coming into ever-new relations as a result:

> [T]he boat is a floating piece of space, a place without a place, that exists by itself, that is closed in on itself and at the same time is given over to the infinity of the sea [...]. [It] is the heterotopia *par excellence*.[13]

Freeman Bentley's works, old and new, are brilliant essays in complex, heterotopic space. They take us into various kinds of space that have analogies to Foucault's ship's interior. Many of these we have noted already: attic spaces, bars and cafes, as well as the lumber rooms and junk shops of her earlier works (like the previously mentioned *Abide*, or *What the Ancients were Commended for* (2010) [p.56]). Sometimes, as in *Passage* (2011) [p.63], the reference to a ship's interior is explicit; it shows us a nautically themed restaurant in the floating city of Venice, itself a giant heterotopia. They are places that seem superficially static, but the artist makes us wonder whether there is a far greater movement at work all around them, which we cannot see.

In contemporary Western life, and quintessentially in cities, there is a vast pressure to turn all space into possessed space, and in this respect to make it uniform space – precisely quantifiable in its physical dimensions, its postcoded location and its market value. Polly and Digory's "in-between places, behind the walls and above the ceilings and under the floor" are assimilated to this new simplicity, whose simpleness is a function of the hungry appropriation of new assets. There is little patience in such a world for what John Ruskin once celebrated in the gothic, namely (in the words of the contemporary theologian John Milbank) "the Christian imperative of straining for the ultimate at the risk of thereby more comprehensively exhibiting one's finite and fallen insufficiency."[14] The reigning dogma of a commercial and utilitarian world is that nothing is to be unaccounted for; that there is no place for anything whose purpose is not easily fixed and costed. There is an antipathy to complexity, and a repression of the heterotopic.

One of the primary stylistic expressions of such dogma, not least in architecture and design, is a certain sort of modernist minimalism. Utility welcomes the most cost-efficient use of (often mass-produced) materials, and simple, clean lines, planes and spaces. Willingly or not, it can easily find itself allied to materialist reductionism (matter without spirit), and the prioritisation of profit or power.

 Previous spread: *To Have and to Hold*, 2010, oil on 4 boards, at The Florence Trust, St. Saviour's, Highbury, 2010

Milbank, following Ruskin, looks to the medieval gothic as a source of opposition to this desire to stamp out every pocket of supposed pointlessness, every fertile area of dead space. In the gothic, we have a religiously humane exemplification of the principle of redundancy: its extravagantly untidy complexity signalling with honesty that humanity cannot impose completeness or finality on its environment, and that our best way of witnessing and relating to the God who alone gathers all things into one – things in heaven and on earth – is by generating a richly-textured abundance of loose ends and ragged edges within an interconnected and evolving architectural organism. A celebration of abundant redundancy is held together with "a balancing sense of unifying form" that is discovered as much as it is imposed,[15] and in which "many altars, many depictions, many procedures" can be enacted within the frame of an "upwardly aspiring building".[16]

The principle of redundancy brings us back to the themes of excess and gratuity with which we began. It also brings us back to Freeman Bentley's work, for, interestingly, the themes Milbank explores through his appreciation of the gothic are strikingly close to those that Freeman Bentley explores not in the gothic specifically, but in the dense interplay of multiple styles none of which is allowed hegemony. Her practice explores different architectural languages, from the gothic (the neo-gothic architecture of St Saviour's, Highbury, for instance [see p.19 and pp.38-9]) to the baroque, to the modernist, with attention to the architecture of the industrial revolution along the way. She shows how these styles form a sort of palimpsest, overlaid one upon another as they often are in urban contexts. No simple statement of intention, no single manifestation of personal, civic or institutional wealth, is allowed to remain unqualified in this complex world.

Freeman Bentley's work thereby represents a kind of resistance to false totalities, to prematurely homogenising political schemes or theories of value or meaning. She asserts that modern ideologies will never eliminate all heterotopias; they can only try to pretend they do not exist. However aggressively they may fight to do so, with dehumanising and spiritually destructive determination, she denies that they will ever finally succeed in making all complex space simple. With an exceptional originality of vision she works to honour the possibilities that lie hidden in (apparent) redundancy. And because the balancing sense of unity that will prevent her overlaying of styles and accumulating of objects turning into a mere heap cannot for her be achieved by a nostalgic reintroduction of medieval hierarchies, she looks for their unity instead in the spirit that binds them. There is a fluidity in her work; an animation of apparently static spaces and contingent objects, which are shown to have a mysterious sort of communion with one another as a result. In their own unique way, these animating bonds do an analogous job to what the medieval gothic did in Ruskin's scheme.

Etymologically, animation is related to the word anima, which is the Latin equivalent of the Greek *psyche* – and so we are returned to another theme with which we began. Freeman Bentley's works show us how ensouled or enspirited matter is in some way being reanimated, and set in motion towards an end we cannot yet see. In Polly's words: "It goes on. I don't know how far." Or in the somewhat less hesitant (but similarly un-final) language of Christian Scripture, "faith is the assurance of things hoped for, the conviction of things not seen."[17] The work of the Holy Spirit in matter – if we discern it – ensures that the things it animates are always in process: they are moving and travelling as the Spirit transforms them, as it refurbishes them, repurposes them, regenerates them. This is not just any mobility, it is the mobility of spiritual renewal.

And in this regard, again, these complex, object-filled spaces are shown to be really about *us*. We are in the wallpaper, the fuel signs, the chandeliers, the shoes, the ship's instruments, the mirrors, the rooms. This is eloquent matter, and these material things are telling us about ourselves.

Our present is marked by mobility, too – at every point. Our styles change; our use of artefacts and spaces changes; our demographics change. Freeman Bentley's work shows us these things, and then goes beyond them to address realities that aren't visible (or showable in rationalised "real" spaces), from attitudes and agendas on personal, political, social and economic levels (the questions of *ethos* we noted earlier), to the fantastical possibilities with which our imaginations destabilise and mobilise the supposedly real, all the way to notions of the spiritual and the divine, which are, for her, ultimate. She poses a catalogue of questions for us about cities, buildings, interiors and objects, about how these signify meaning on many levels, about how these meanings become ever more complicated over time as they are adapted and used in different ways, and about how part of what they signify may exceed time itself. With her eyes open to these many ideas and issues, she endeavours to make sense of the places she is studying by identifying what factors are at play in any given place, and always with a view to seeking out God's unseen reality at the points where matter becomes transparent to spirit.

For Anna Freeman Bentley, the mobile present harbours intimations of a future that abides, in which corruptible bodies become incorruptible and the world is transformed. In the glimpses of grandeur she offers, we sense, perhaps, the gates of heaven. The present may be mobility, but the future could be glory.

1
T.J. Gorringe, *A Theology of the Built Environment: Justice, Empowerment, Redemption* (Cambridge University Press, 2002), 18.

2
Jacques Maritain, *Creative Intuition in Art and Poetry* (Princeton University Press, 1953), 127; used importantly by Rowan Williams in *Grace and Necessity: Reflections on Art and Love* (London: Bloomsbury, 2006).

3
David Harvey, *The Urban Experience* (Oxford: Blackwell, 1989), 229.

4
Gorringe 2002, 143.

5
Gorringe 2002, 140.

6
Gorringe 2002, 157; citing Hedley Smyth, 'Running the Gauntlet' in M. Jenks, E. Burton and K. Williams (eds), *The Compact City: A Sustainable Urban Form?* (London: Routledge, 1998), 103, 107.

7
Gorringe 2002, 149.

8
Peter Hall, *Cities in Civilization* (London: Weidenfeld and Nicolson, 1998), 285.

9
Hall 1998, 286.

10
1 Corinthians 13:12.

11
C.S. Lewis, *The Magician's Nephew* (London: William Collins and Co., 1980 [1955]), 12, 13-14.

12
Lewis 1980, 37.

13
Michel Foucault, 'Of Other Places' in *Diacritics* 16 (Spring 1986), 27.

14
John Milbank, 'On Complex Space' in *The Word Made Strange: Theology, Language, Culture* (Oxford: Blackwell, 1997), 276.

15
Milbank 1997, 277.

16
Milbank 1997, 278.

17
Hebrews 11:1.

Works

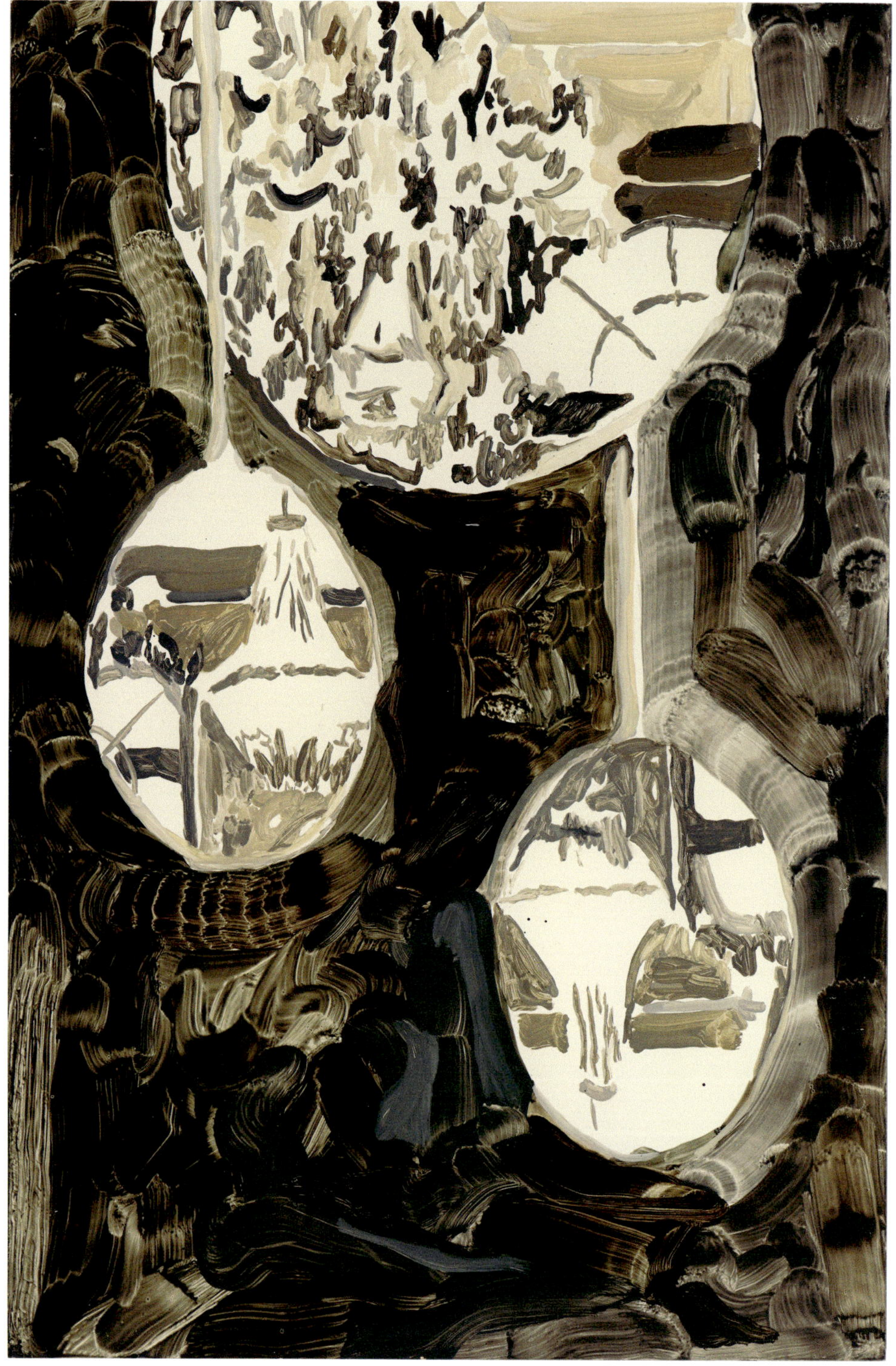

Recollect Revisited, 2008, oil on board, 140 × 90 cm

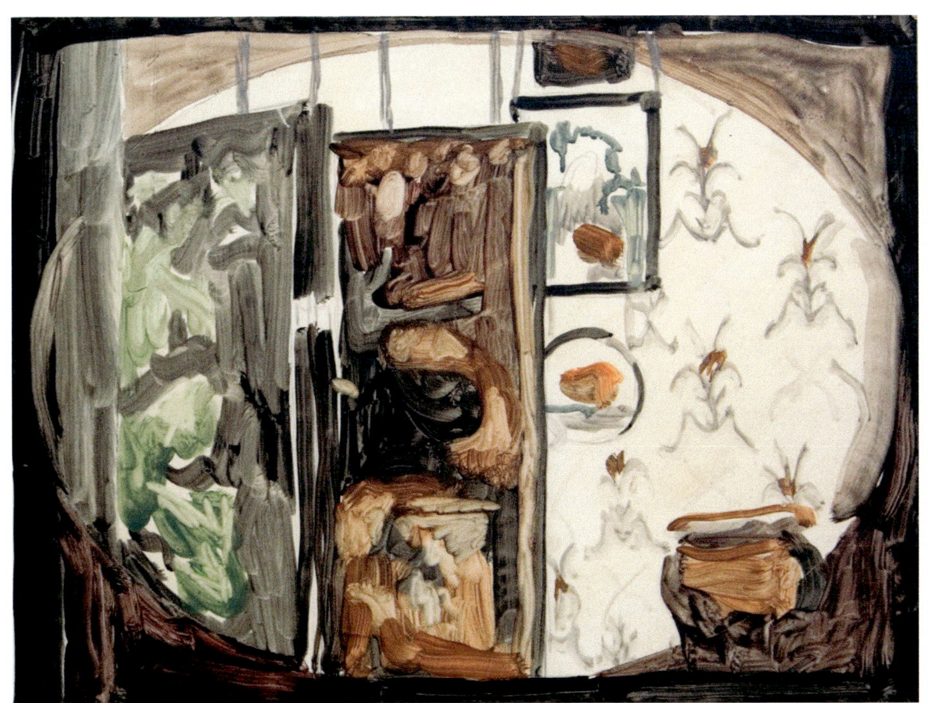

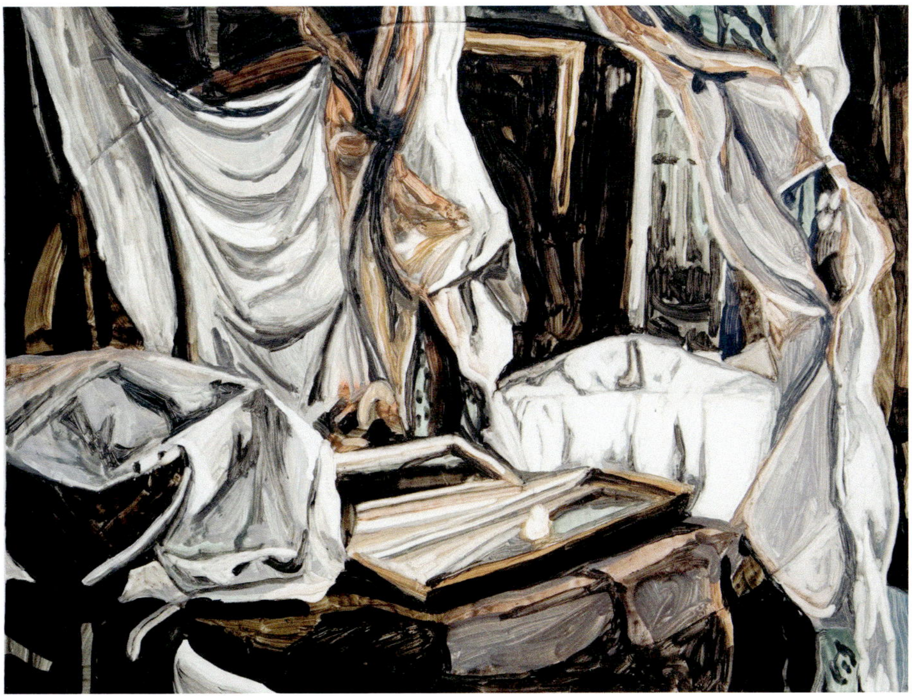

The Screening, 2009, oil on board, 29 × 39 cm   *The Covering*, 2009, oil on board, 30 × 40 cm   45

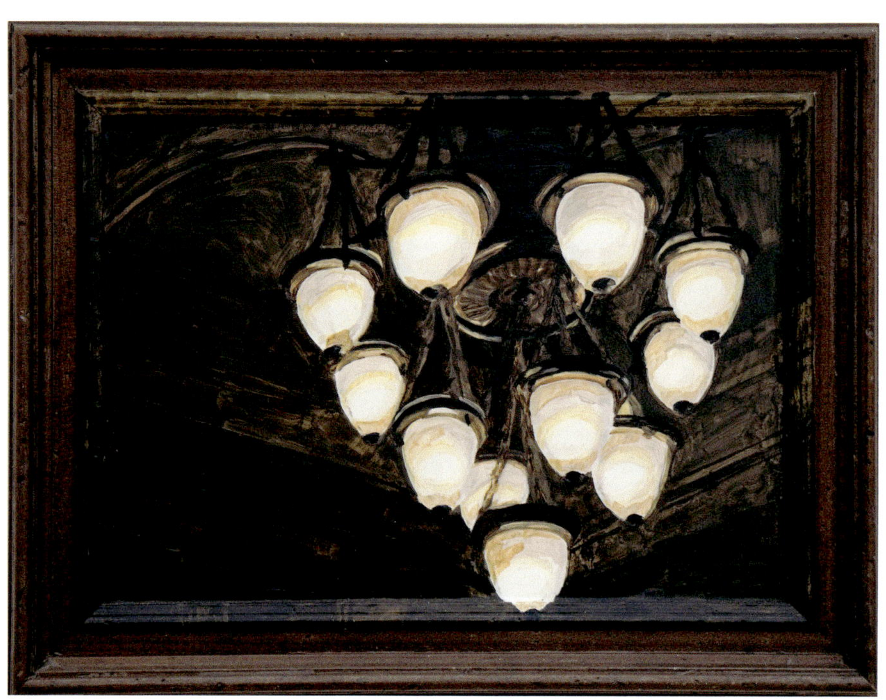

  Framed Light, 2009, oil on board with frame, 35 × 47 cm

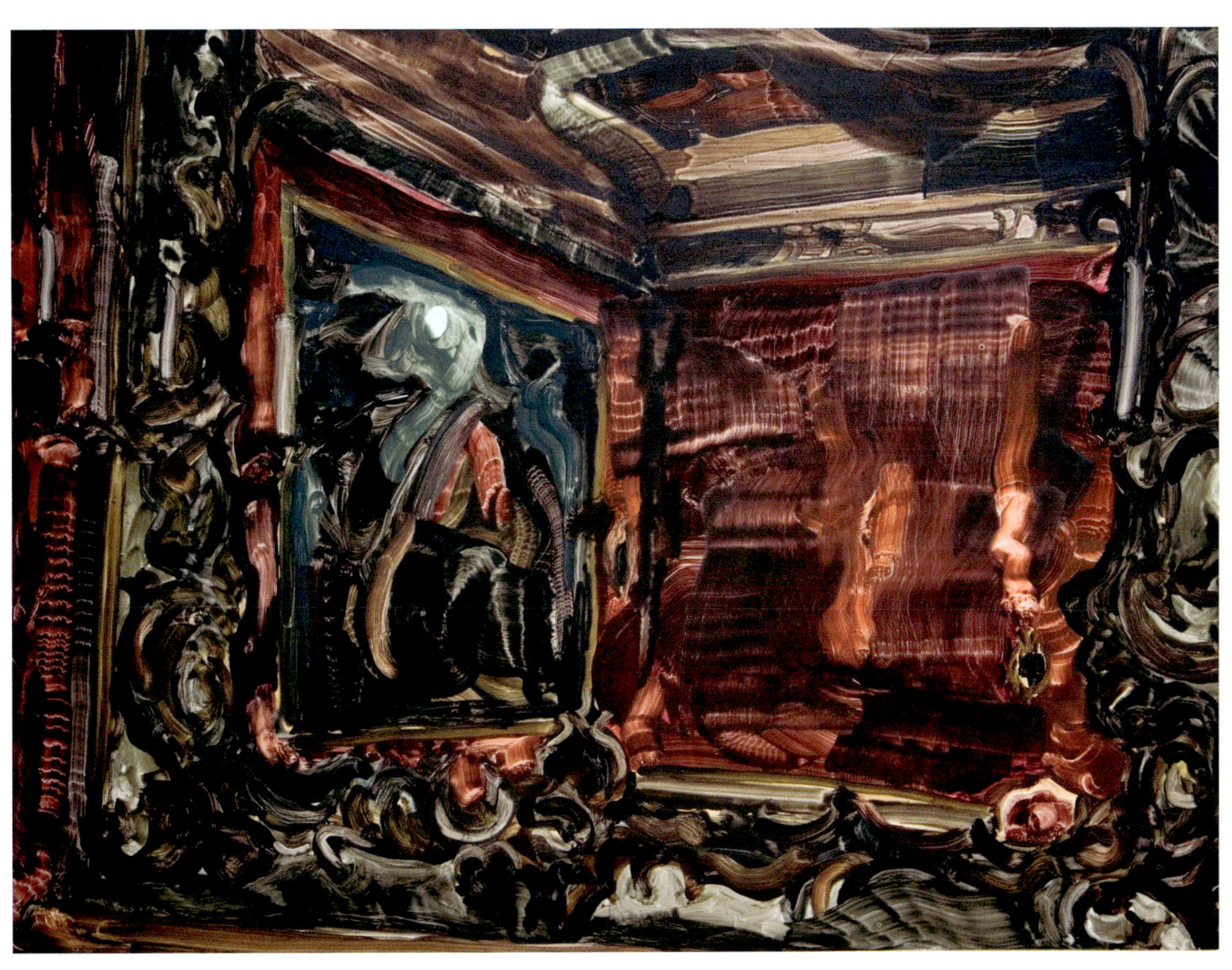

Misshapen Pearl II, 2009, oil on board, 100 × 140 cm

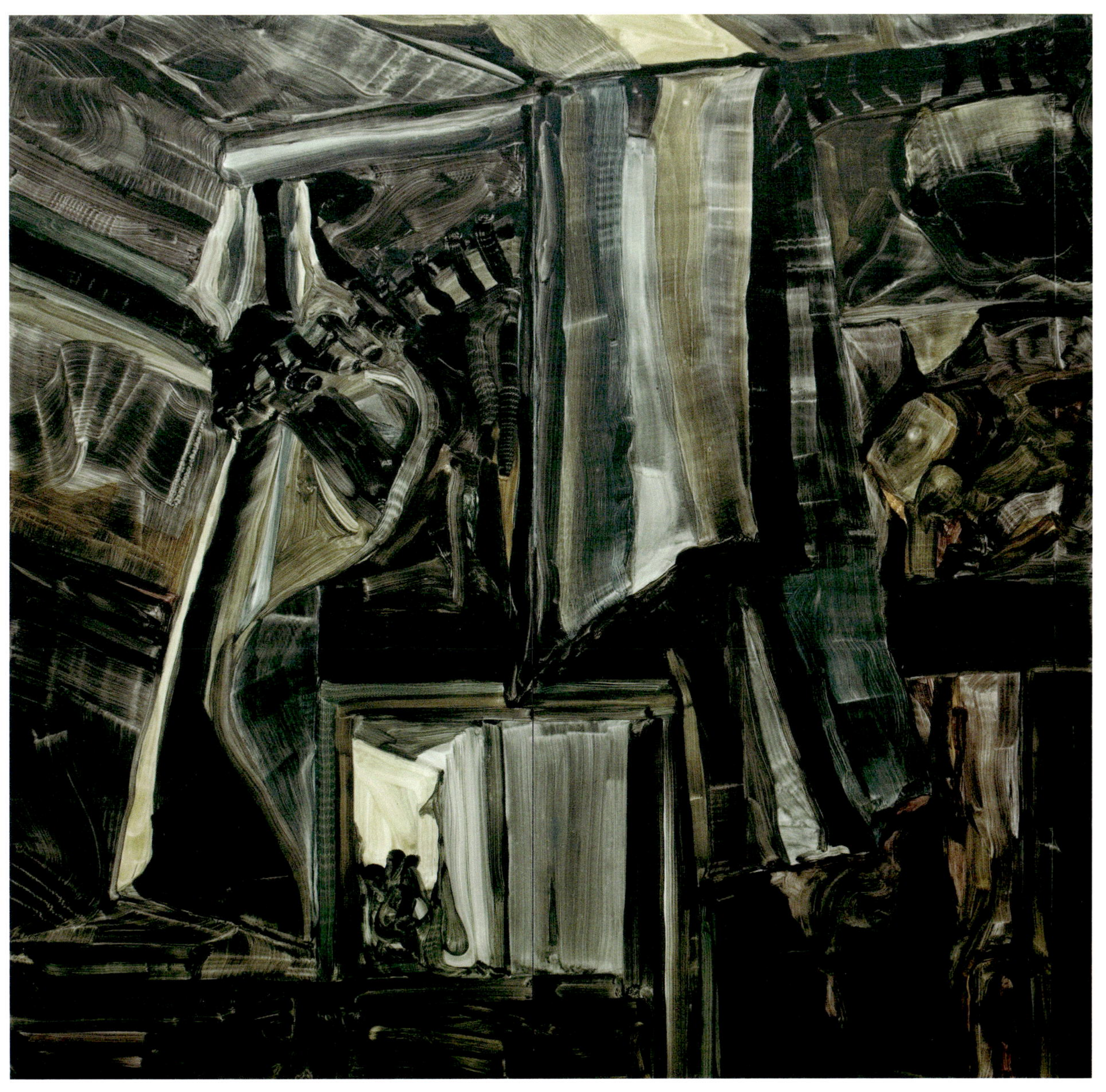

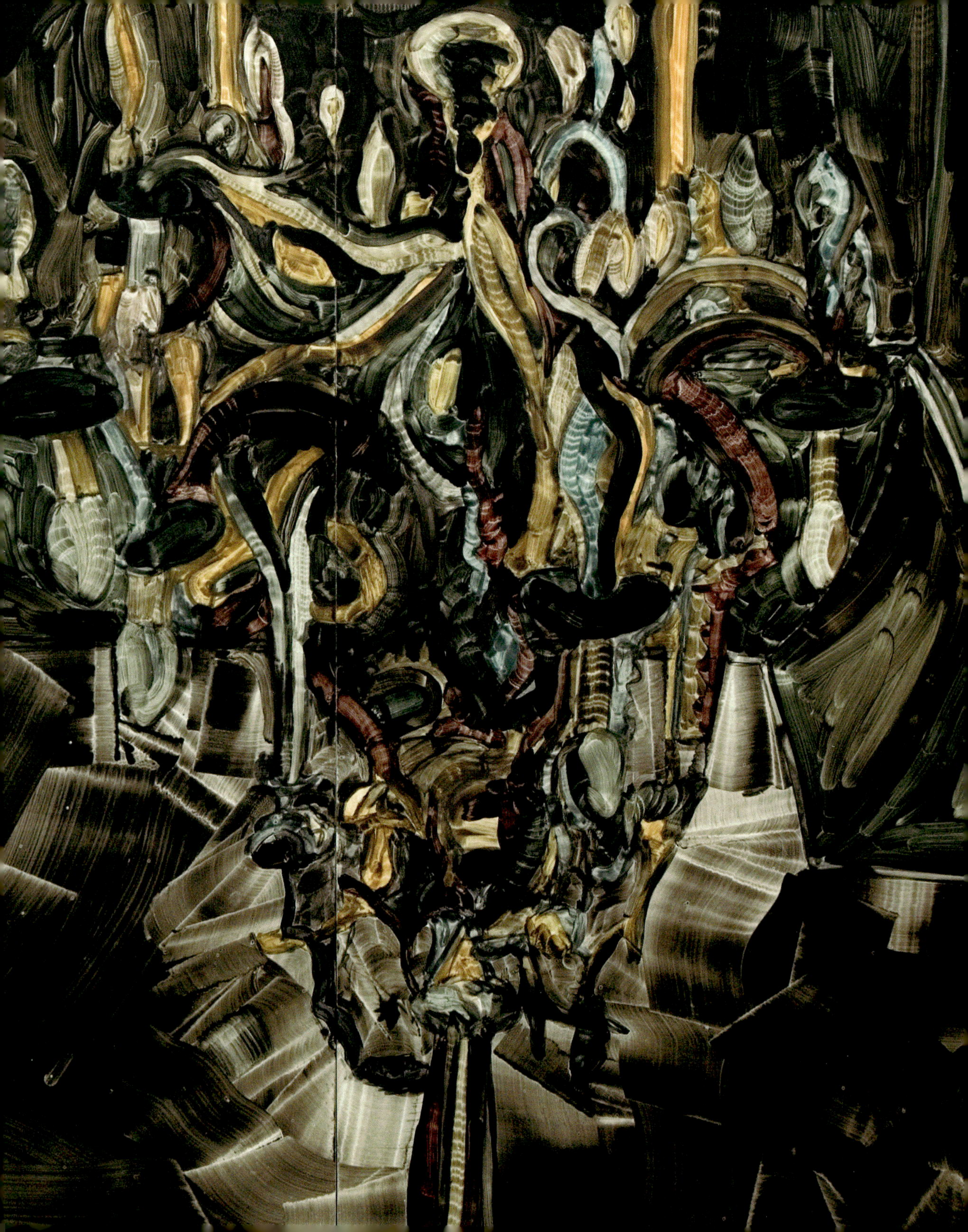

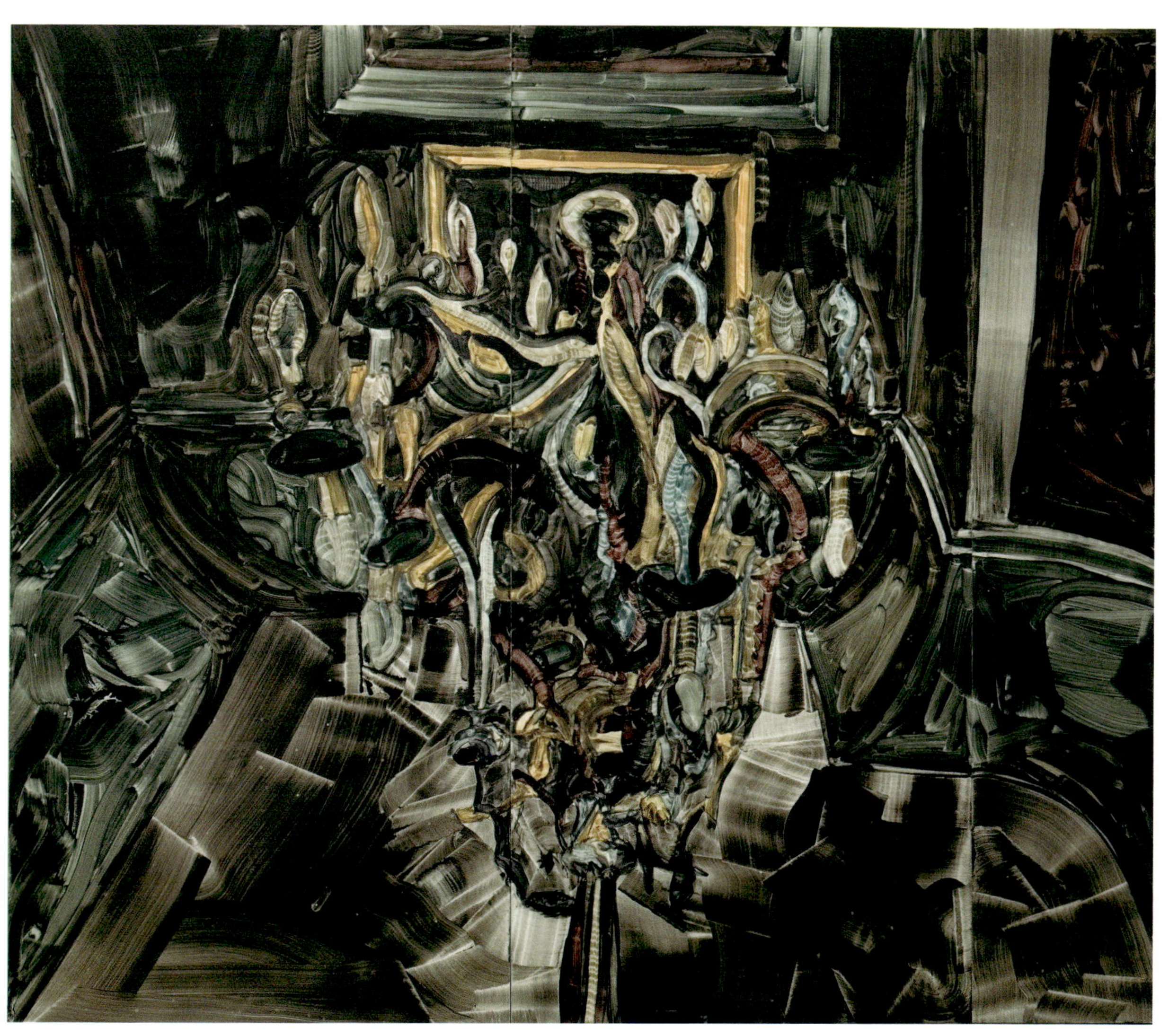

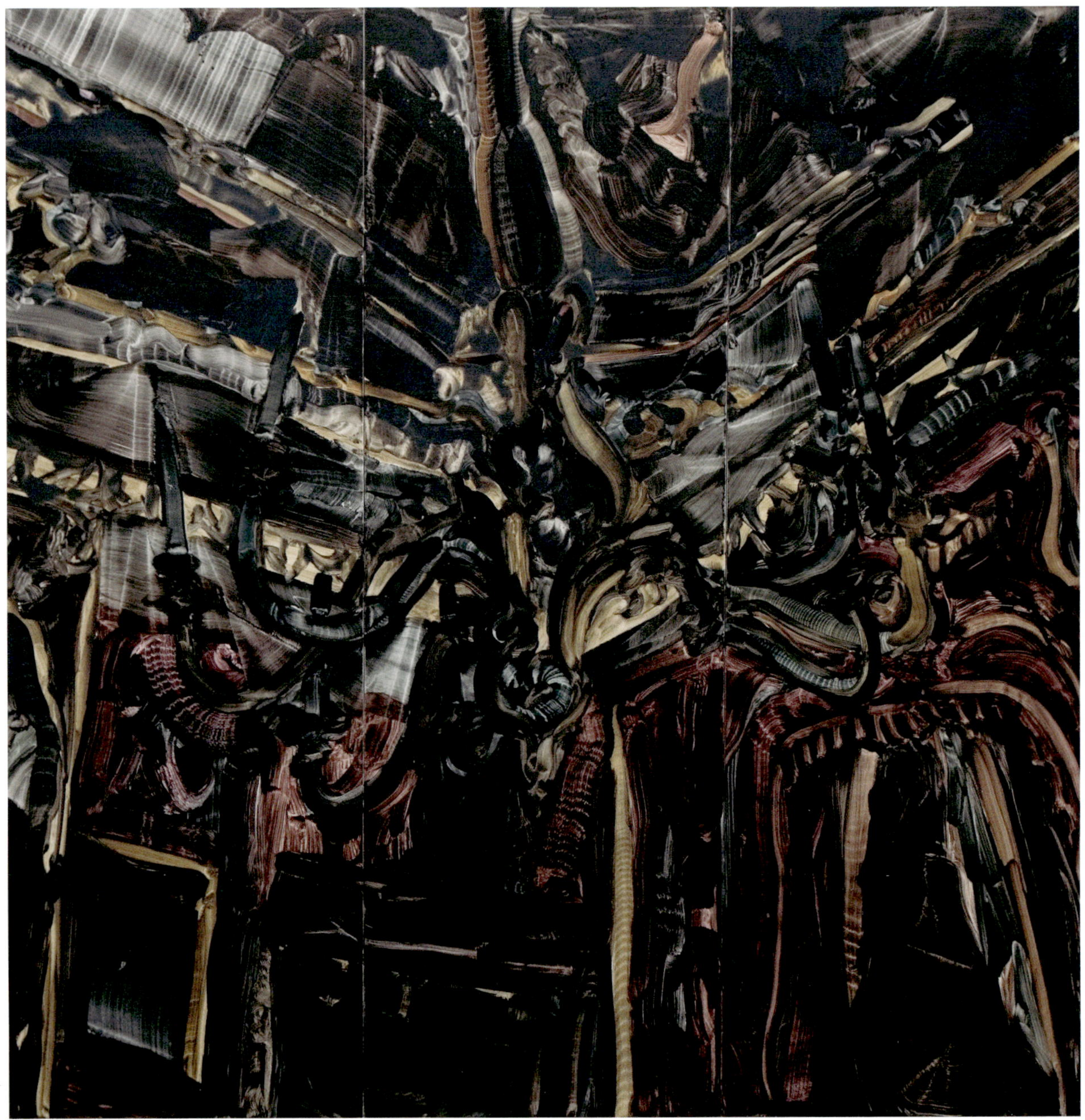

   The People Walking in the Darkness, 2009, oil on board (3 panels), 220 × 210 cm (total)

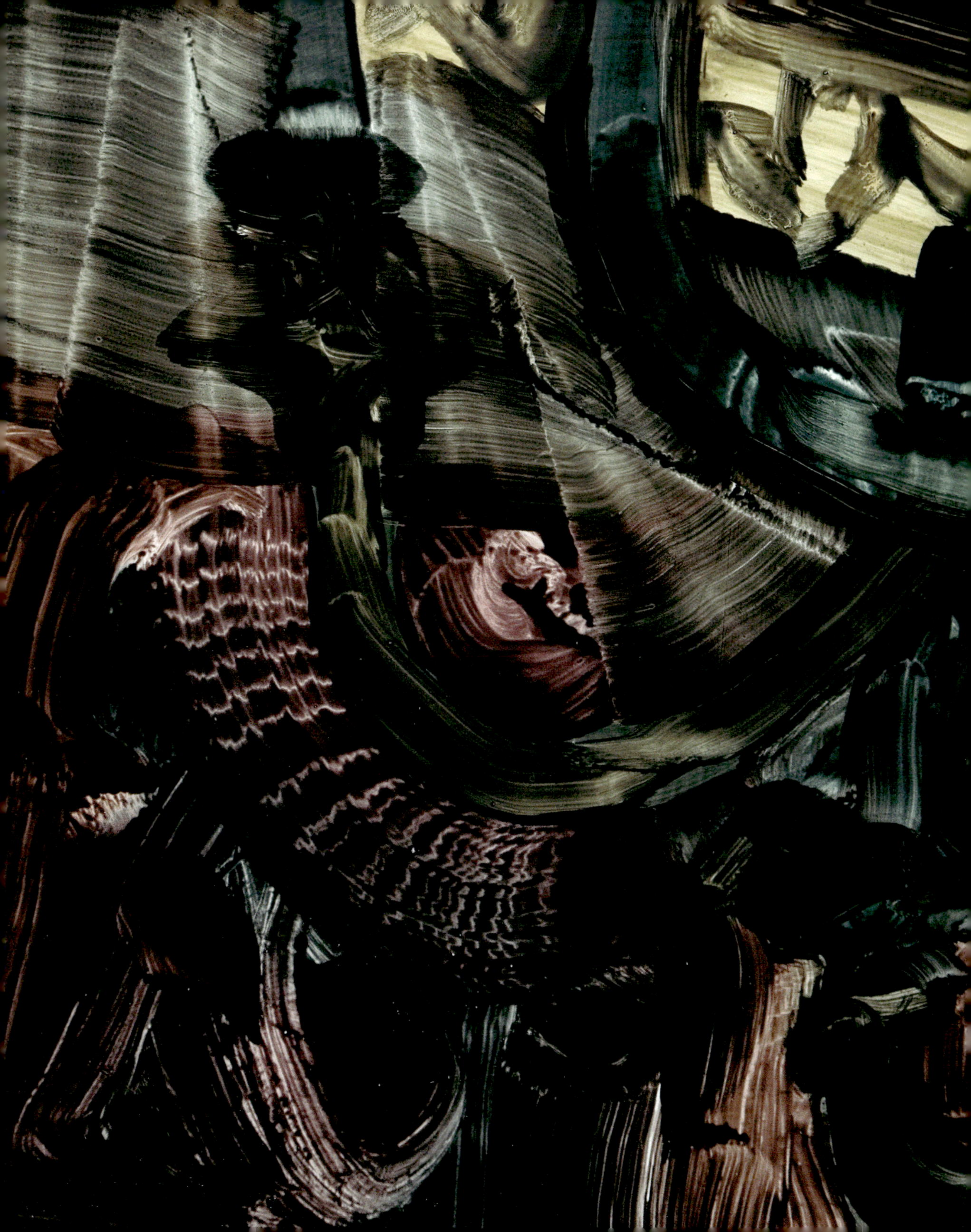

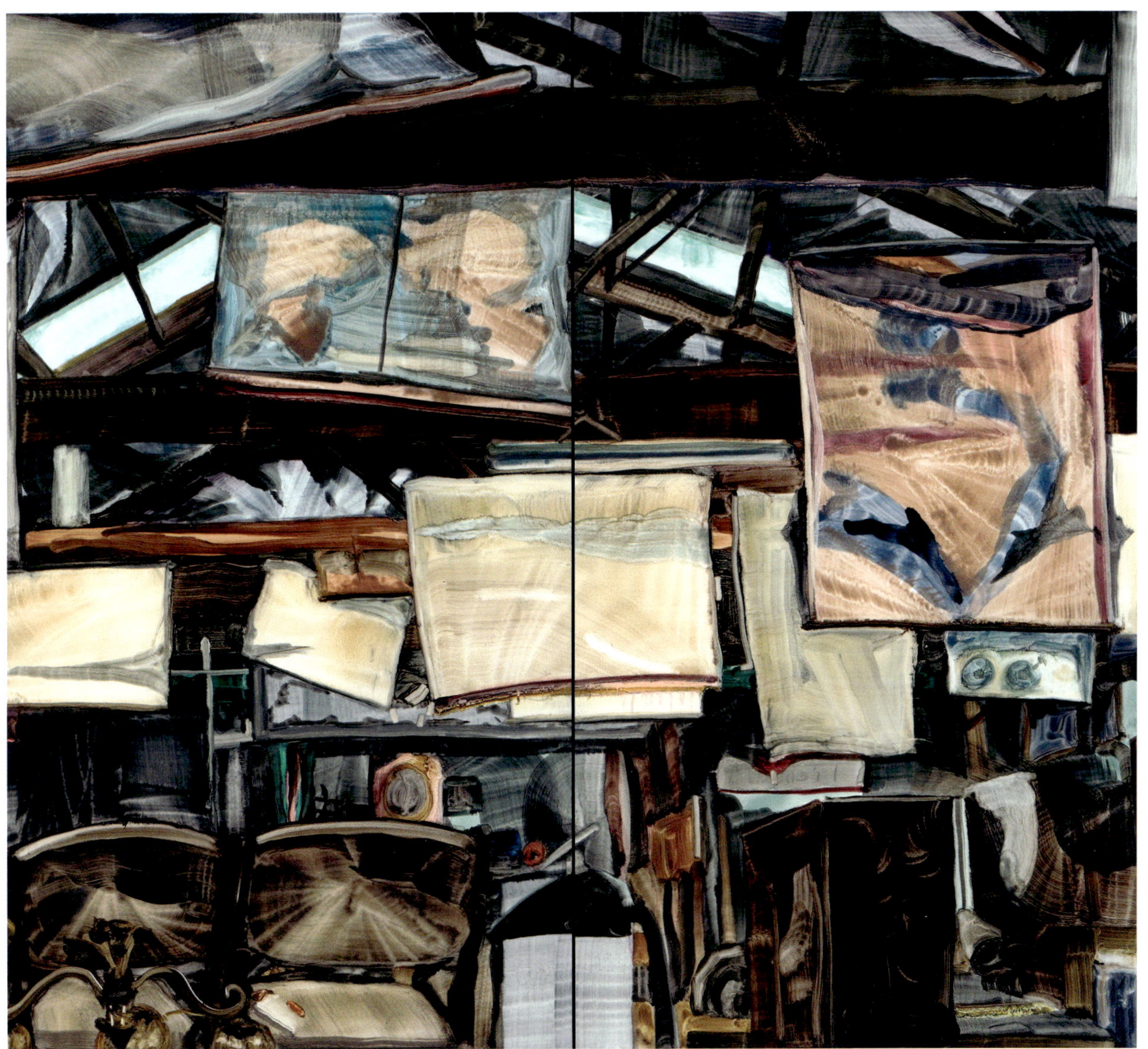

Waiting Silently, 2011, oil on board, 160 × 180 cm (2 panels, 160 × 90 cm each)

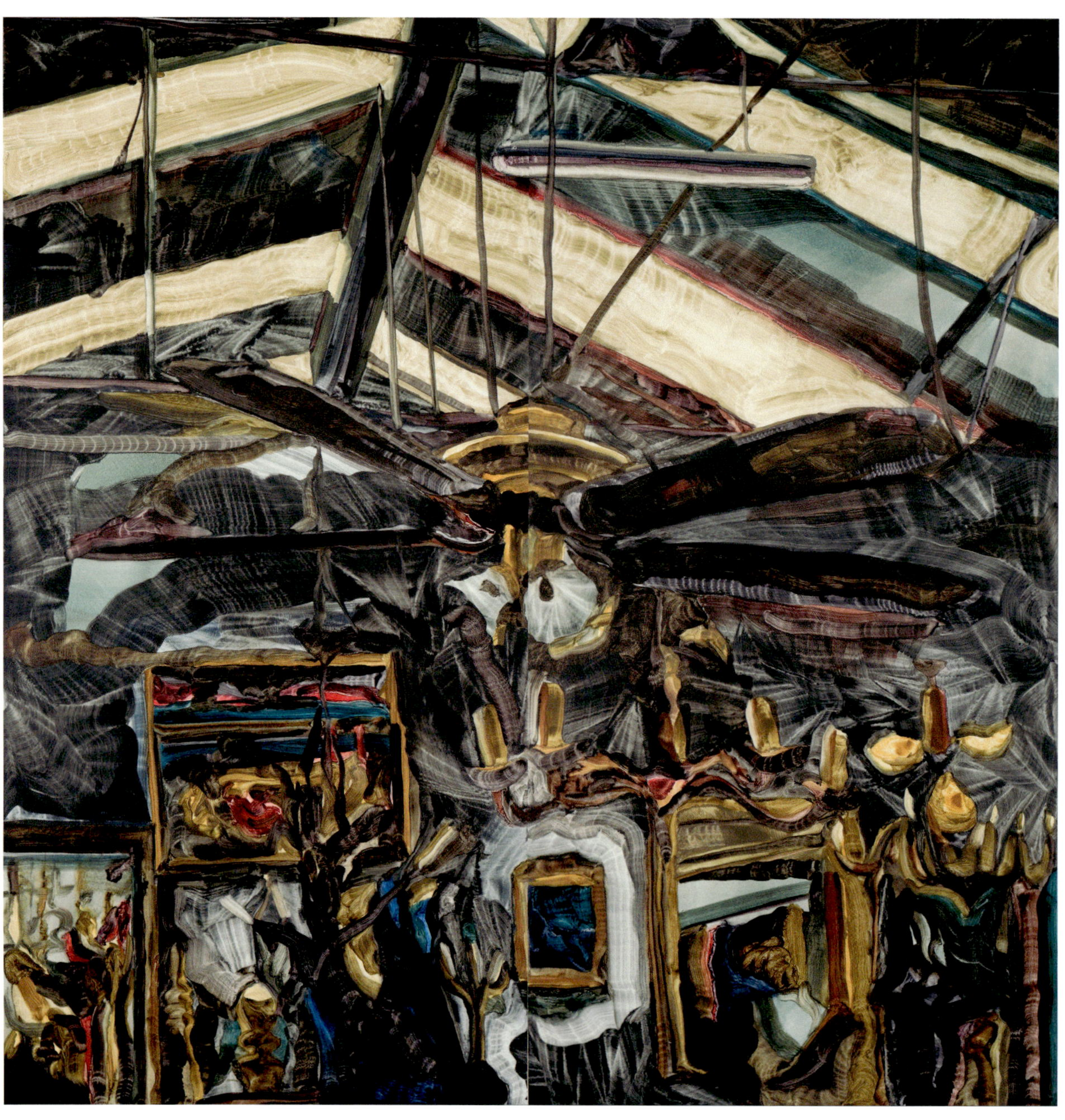

  What the Ancients were Commended for, 2010, oil on board, 244 × 244 cm (2 panels, 244 × 122 cm each)

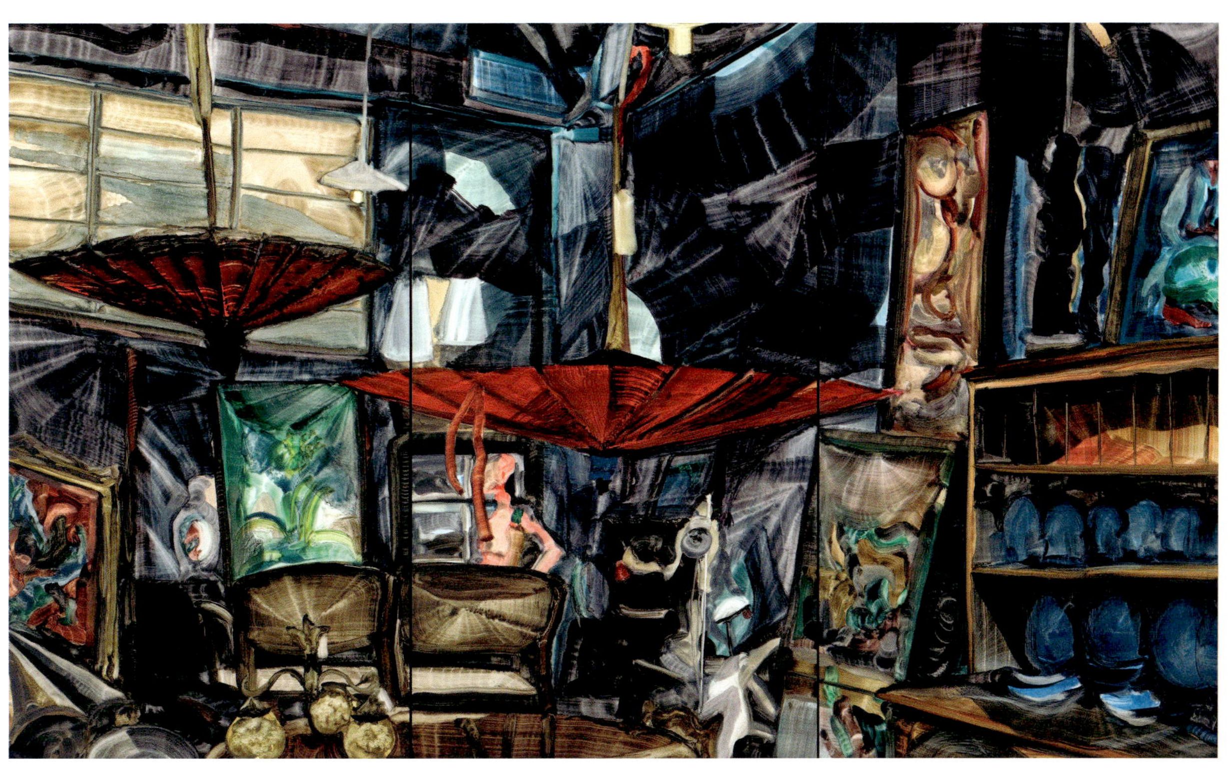

Waiting Hopefully, 2011, oil on board, 160 × 270 cm
(3 panels, 160 × 90 cm each)

Overleaf:
Remain, 2010, oil on aluminium, 20 × 30 cm

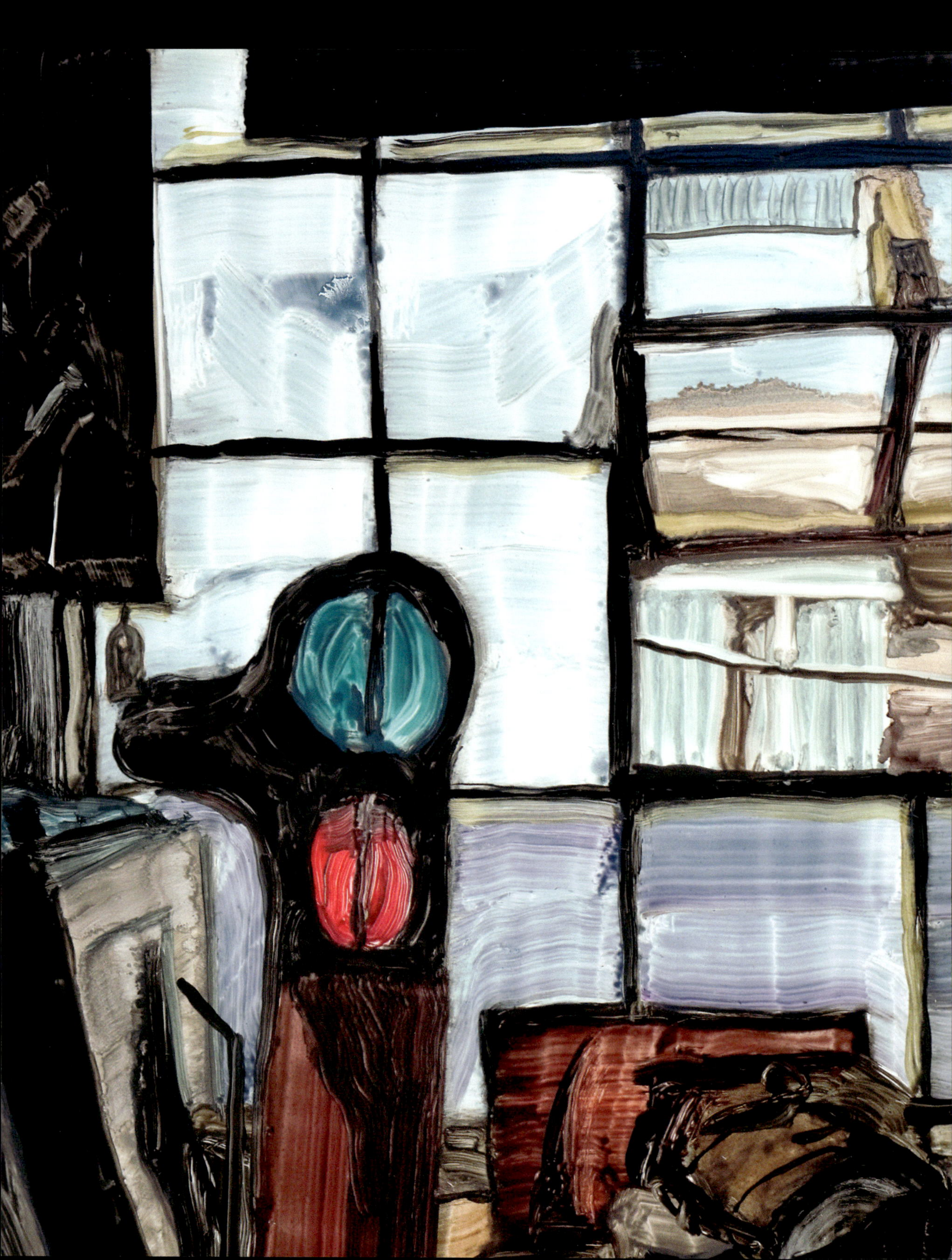

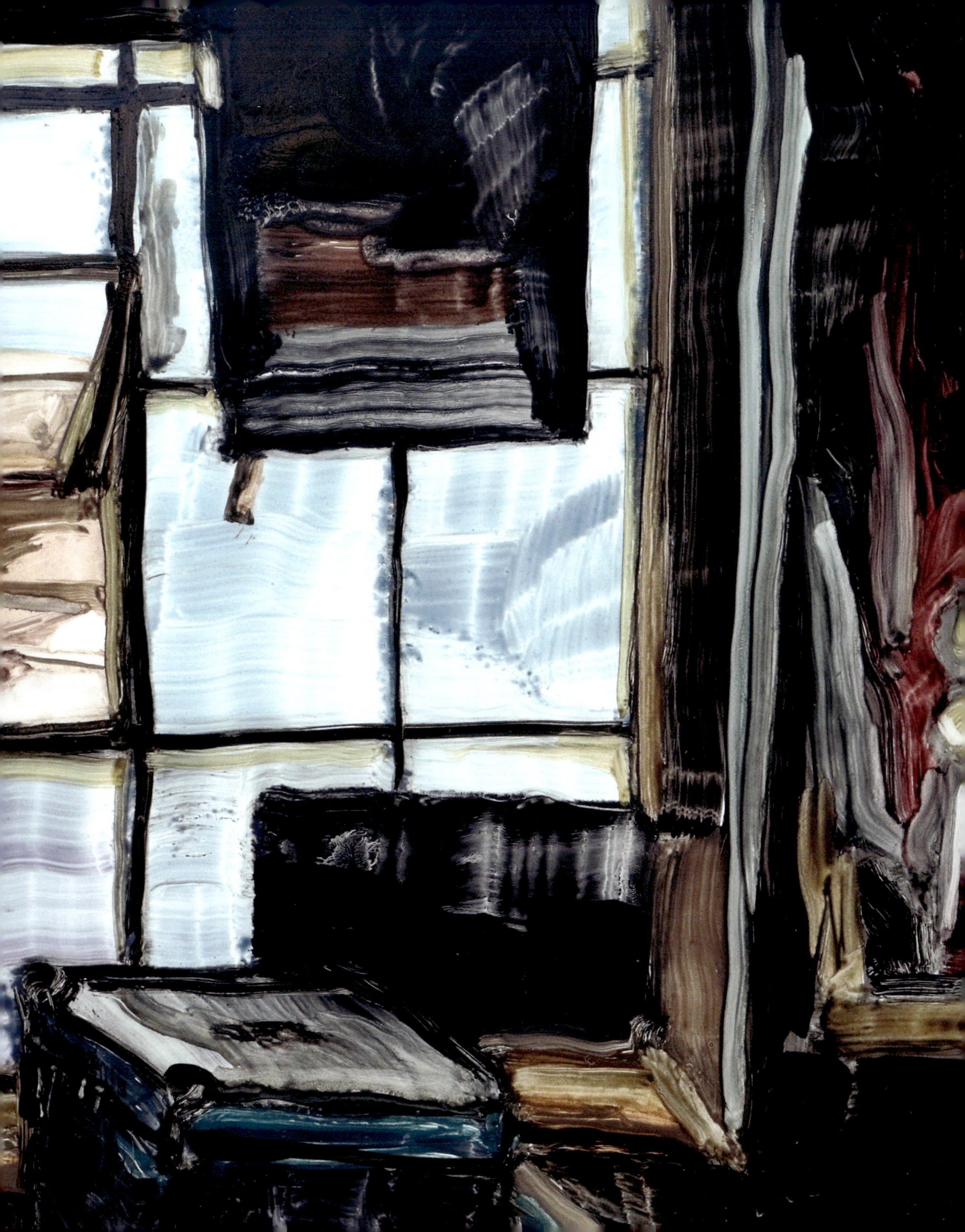

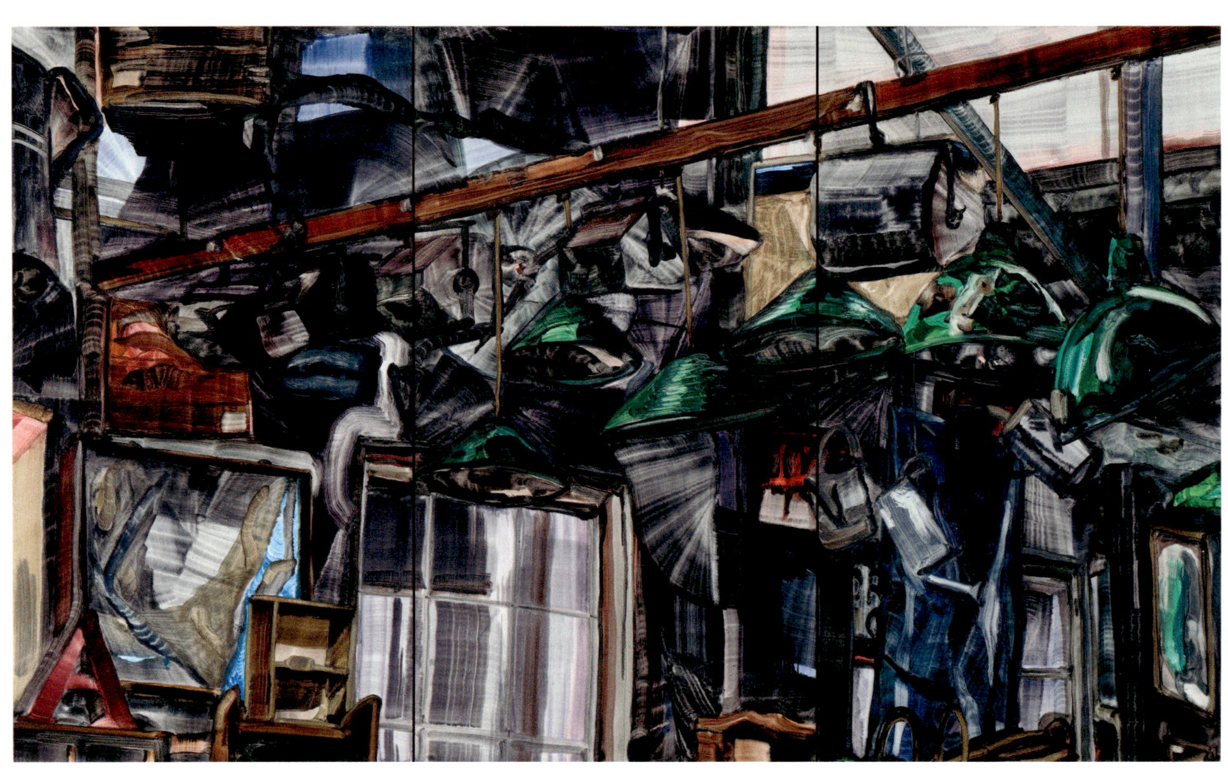

60 *Waiting Anxiously*, 2011, oil on board, 160 × 270 cm (3 panels, 160 × 90 cm each)

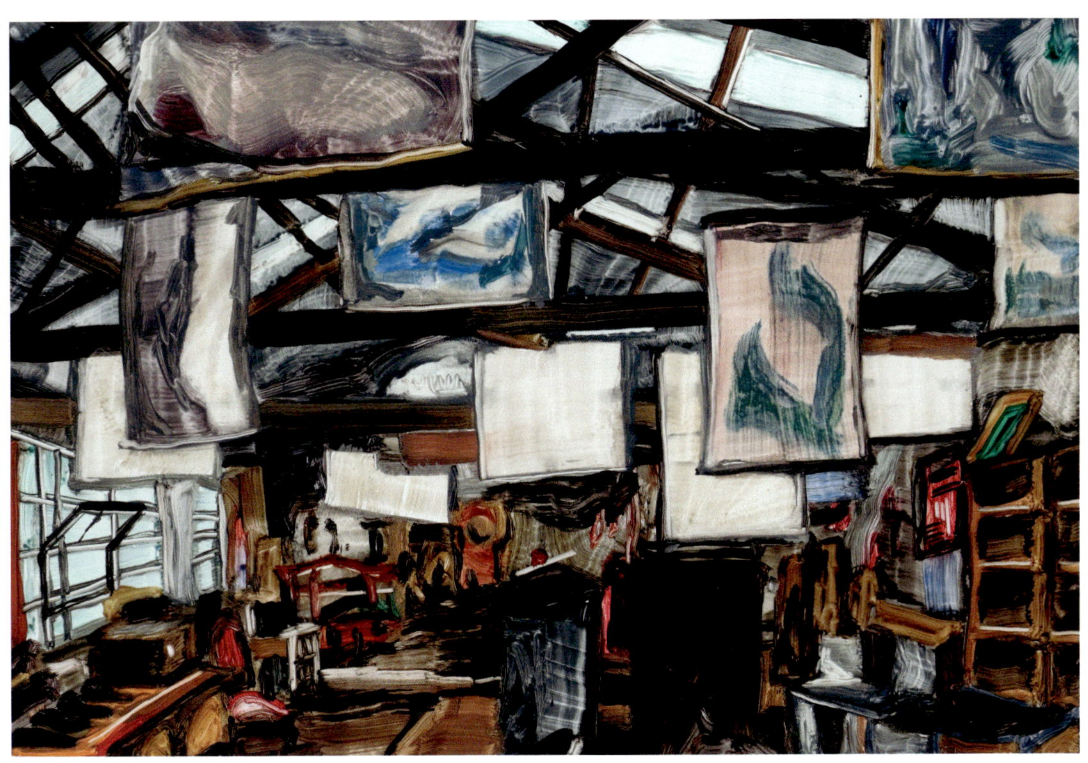

Hang, 2011, oil on aluminium, 20 × 30 cm

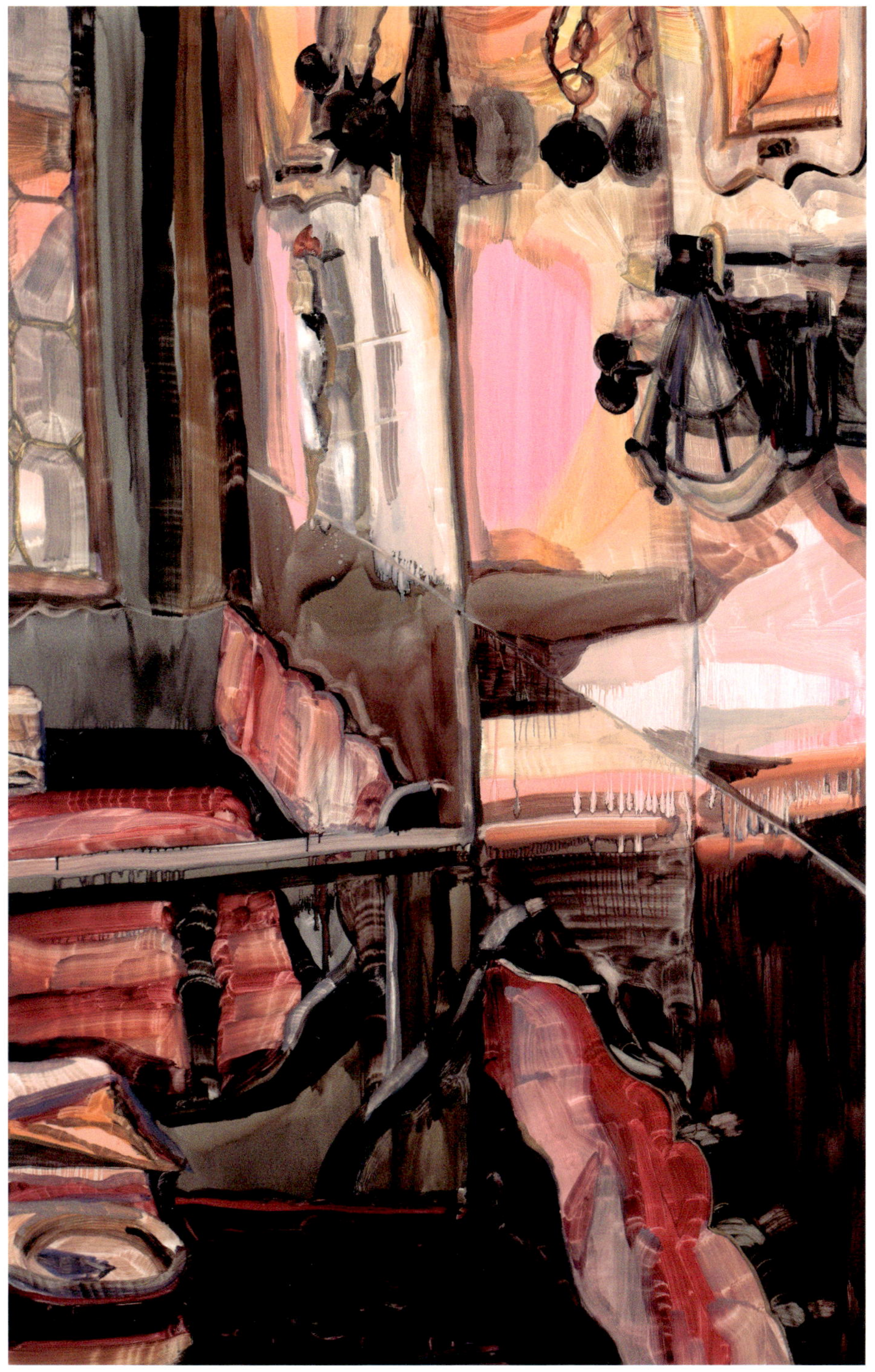

Passage, 2011, oil on board, 180 × 117 cm

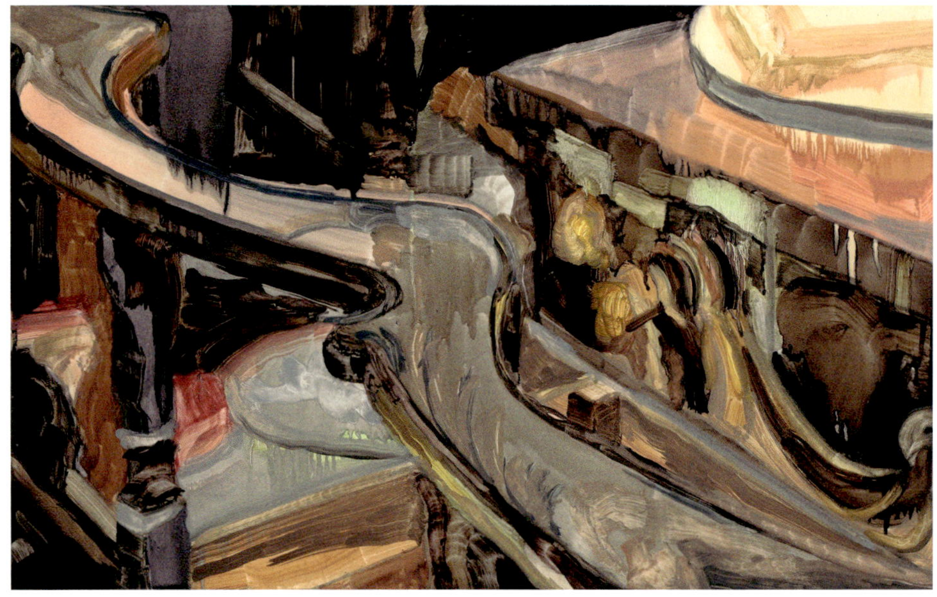

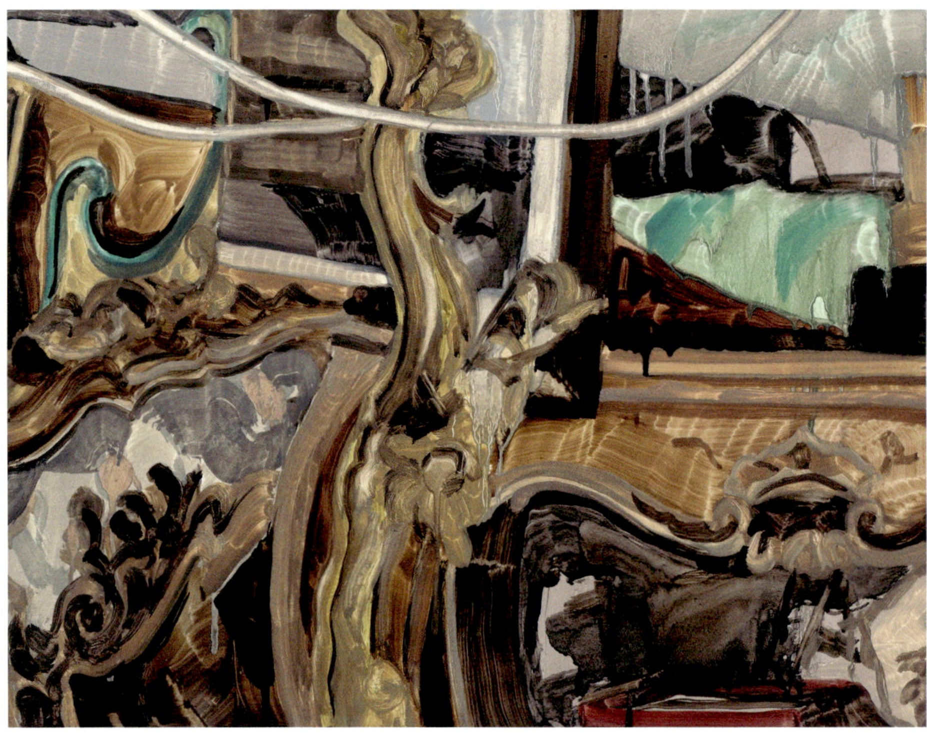

64 *Carved to Adorn a Palace*, 2011, oil on board, 37 × 60 cm   *Hammered Gold*, 2011, oil on board, 40 × 52.5 cm

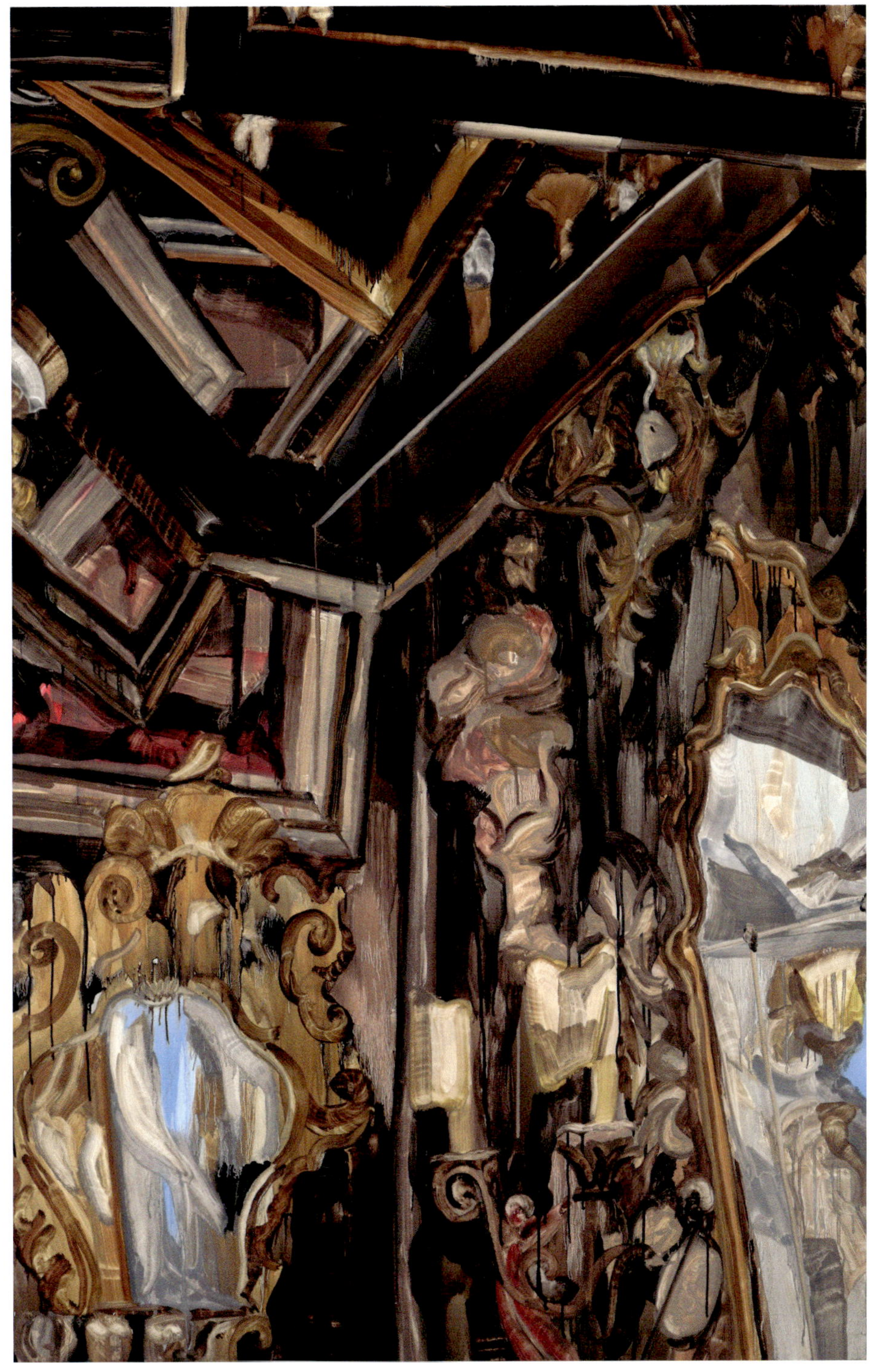

Under the Cloud, 2011, oil on board, 180 × 117 cm

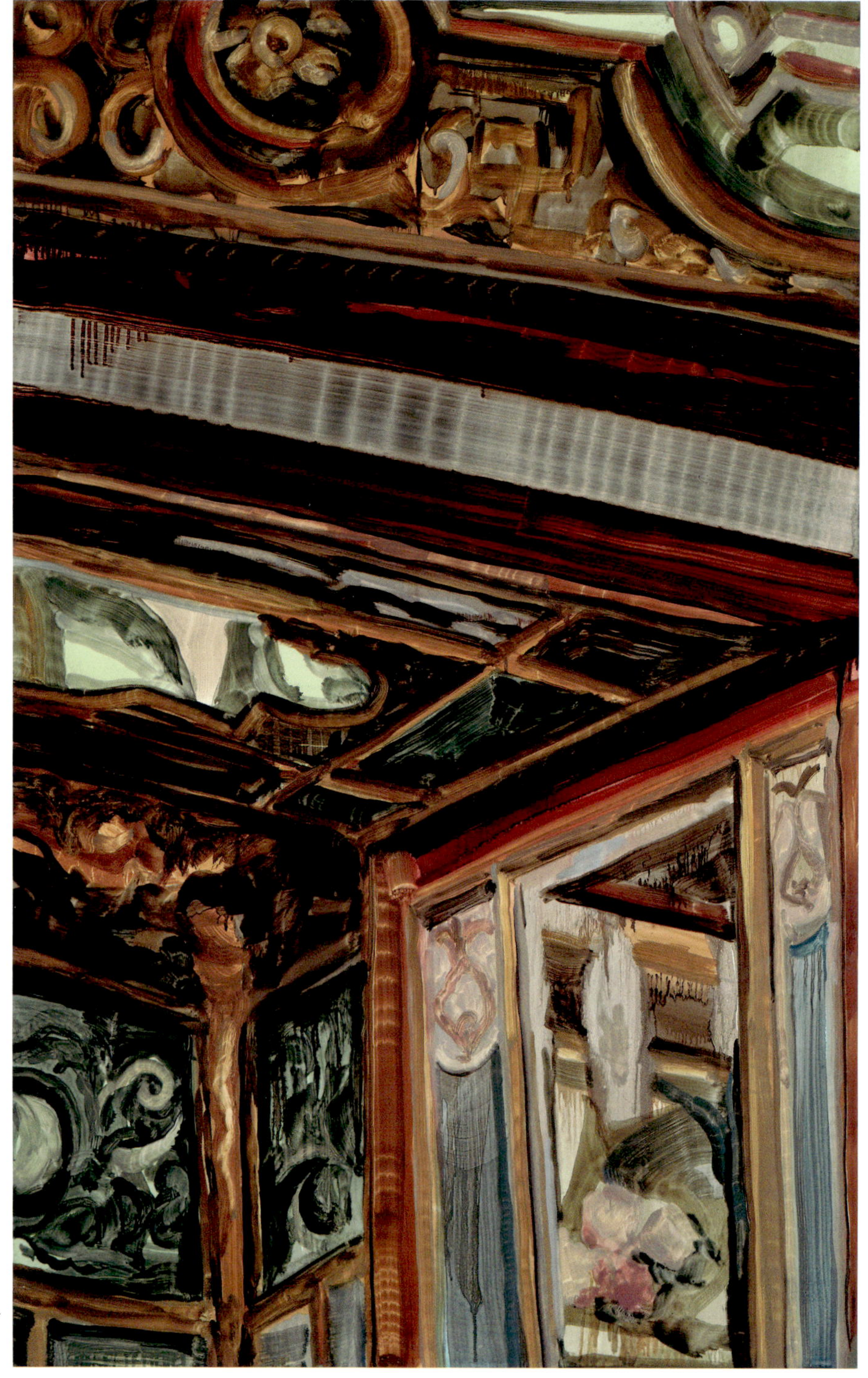

Lobby, 2011, oil on board, 122 × 78 cm

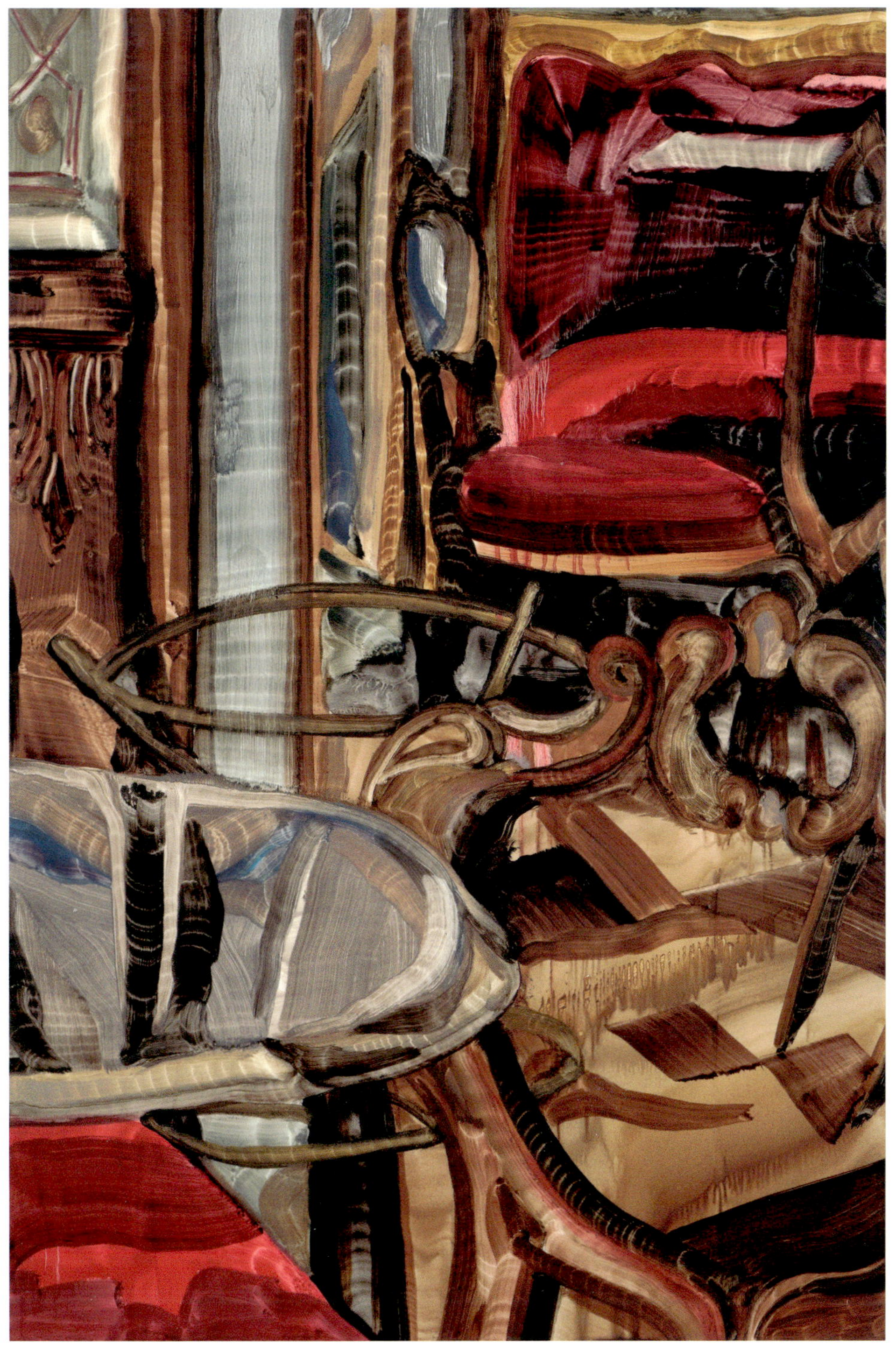

Hall, 2011, oil on board, 120 × 80 cm

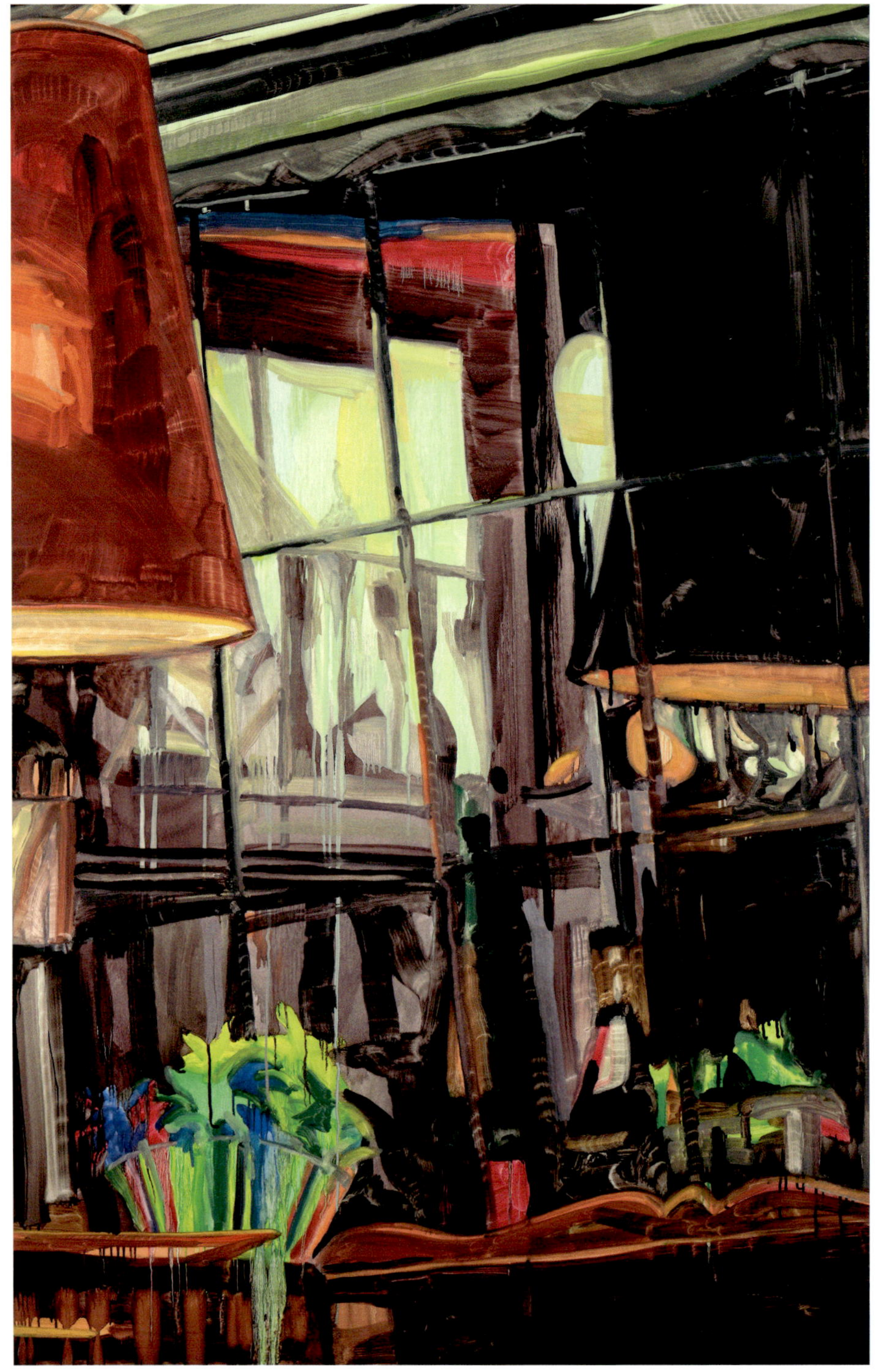

Vacating, 2011, oil on board, 180 × 117 cm

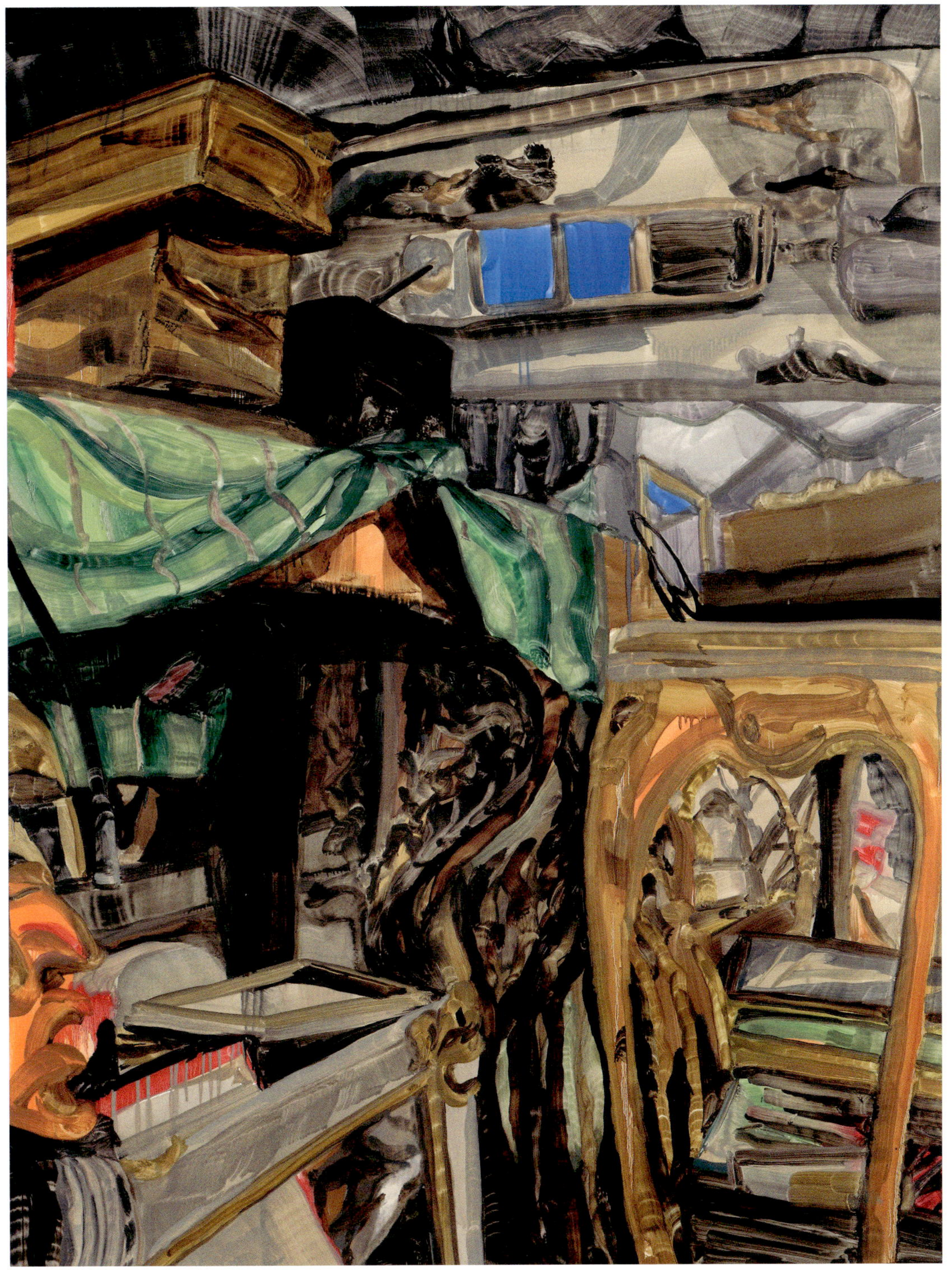

Flattery, 2011, oil on board, 160 × 122 cm

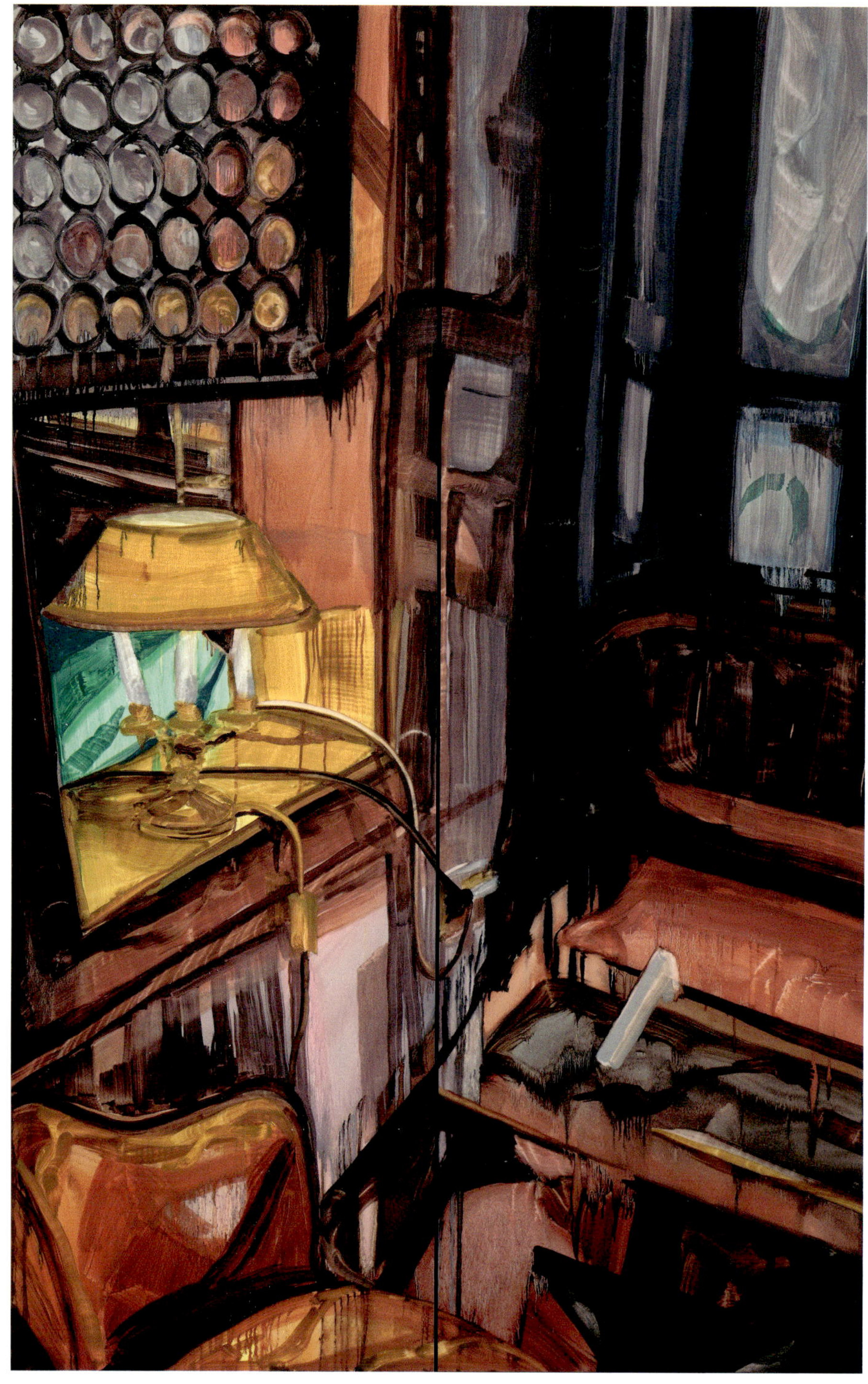

 Darkness Passing, 2011, oil on board, 170 × 110 cm (2 panels, 170 × 55 cm each)

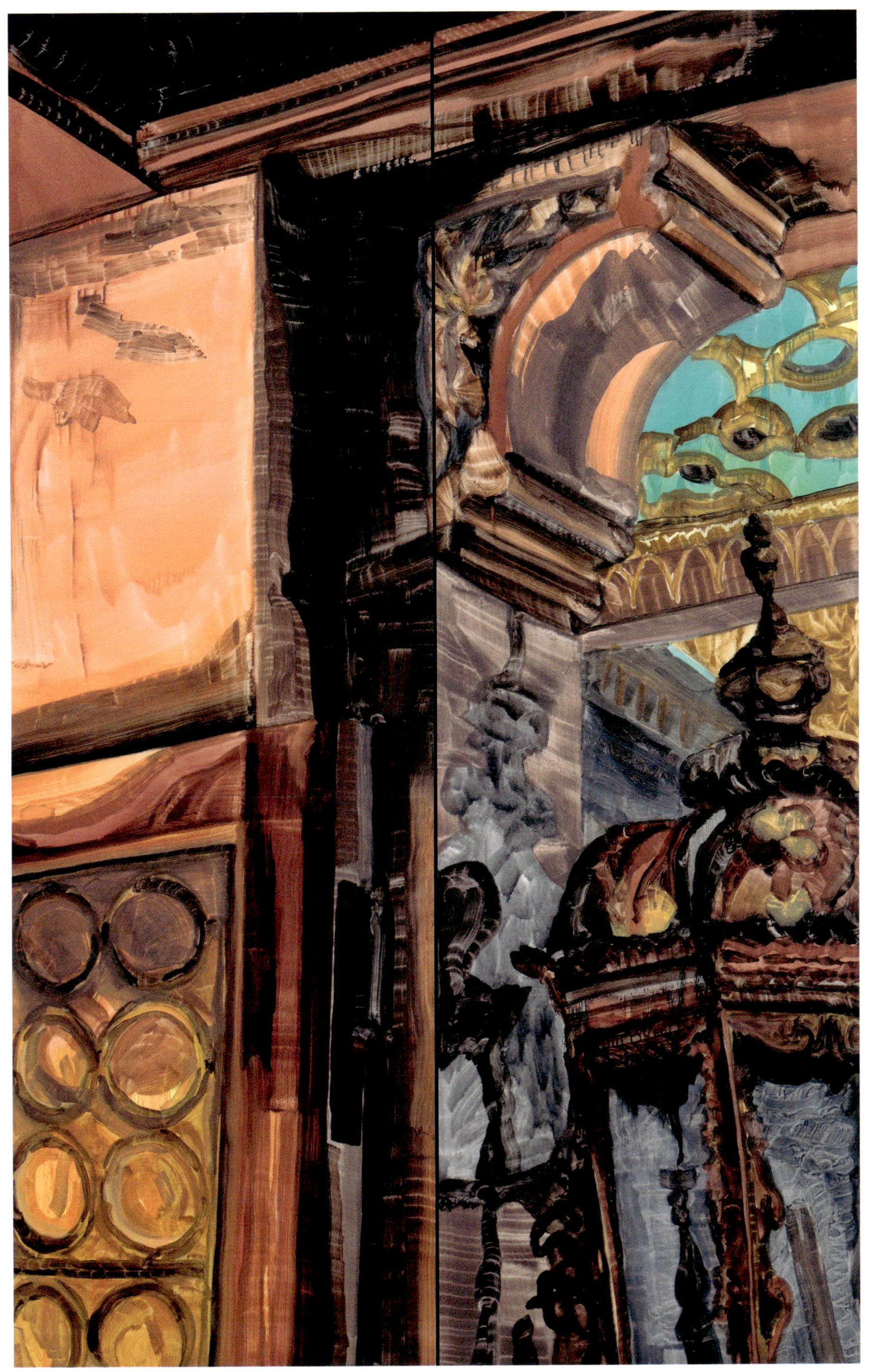

Does not Return, 2011, oil on board, 170 × 110 cm (2 panels, 170 × 55 cm each)

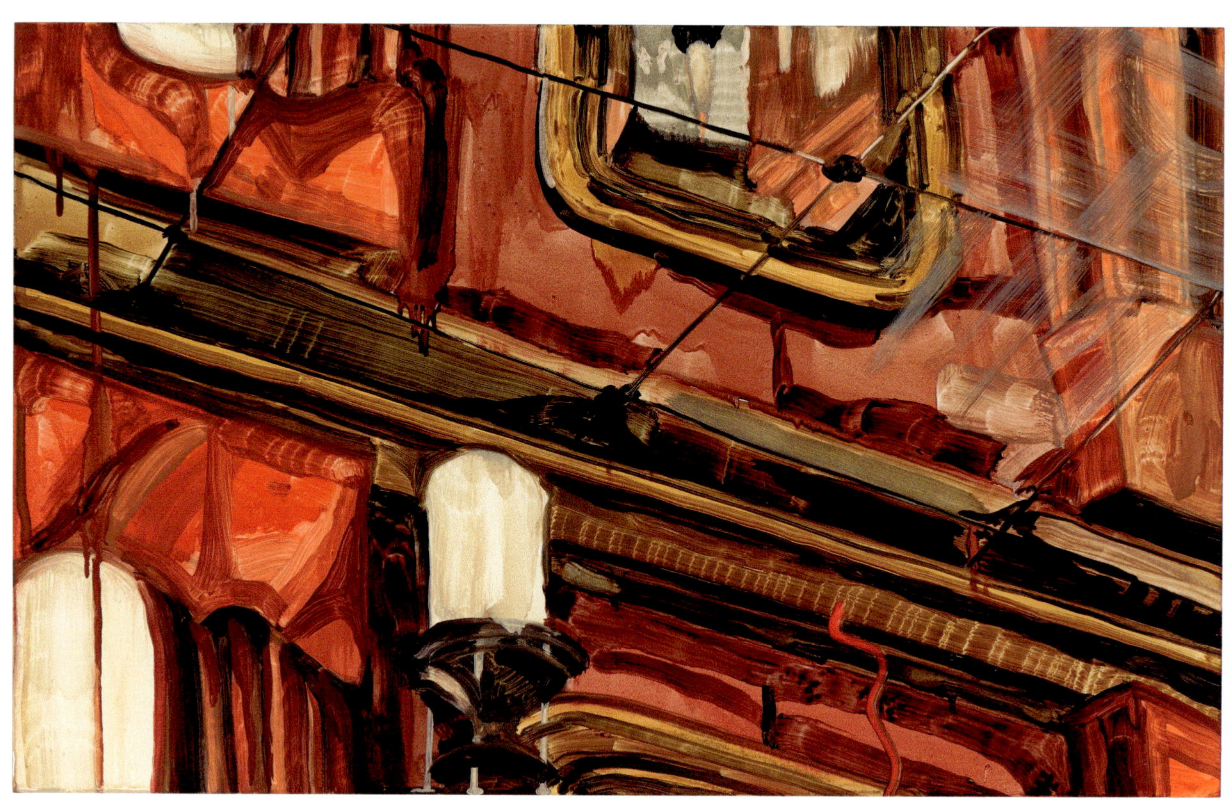

Romantico, 2012, oil on board, 37 × 60 cm

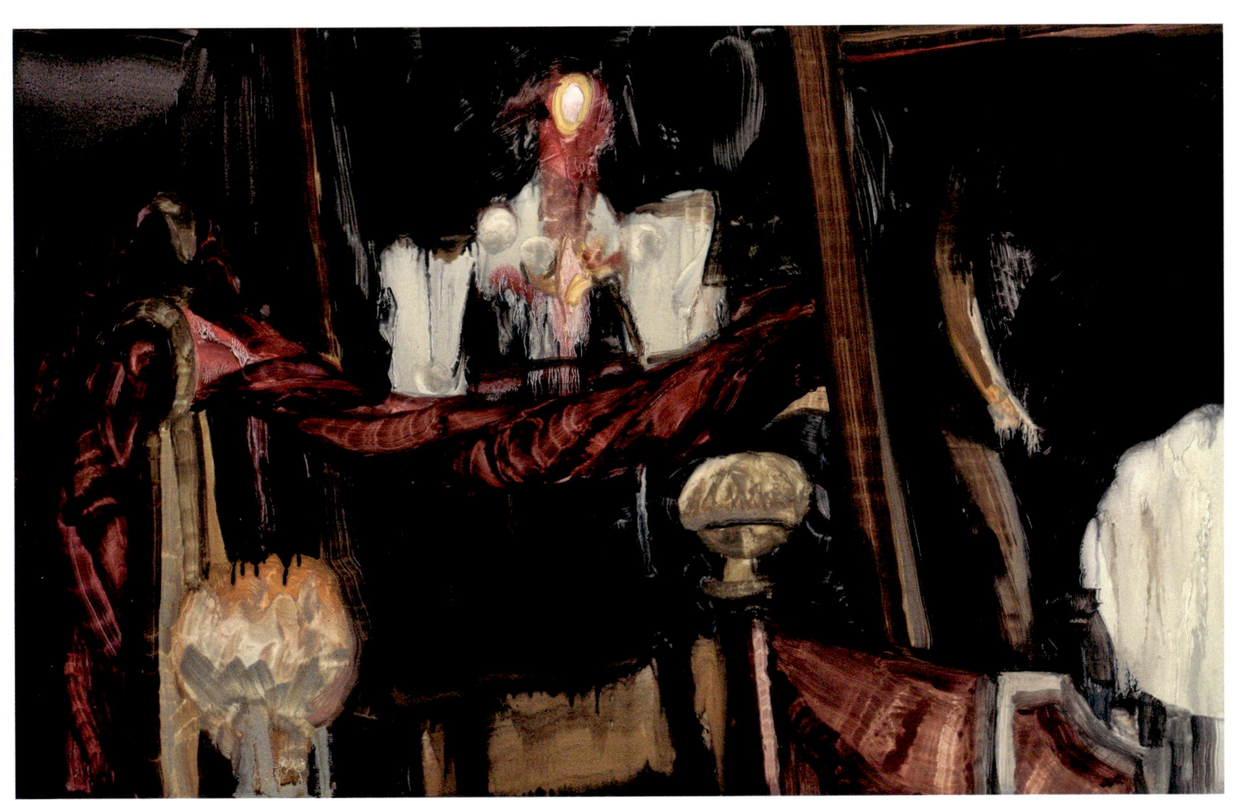

Fleeting Shadow, 2011, oil on board, 37 × 60 cm

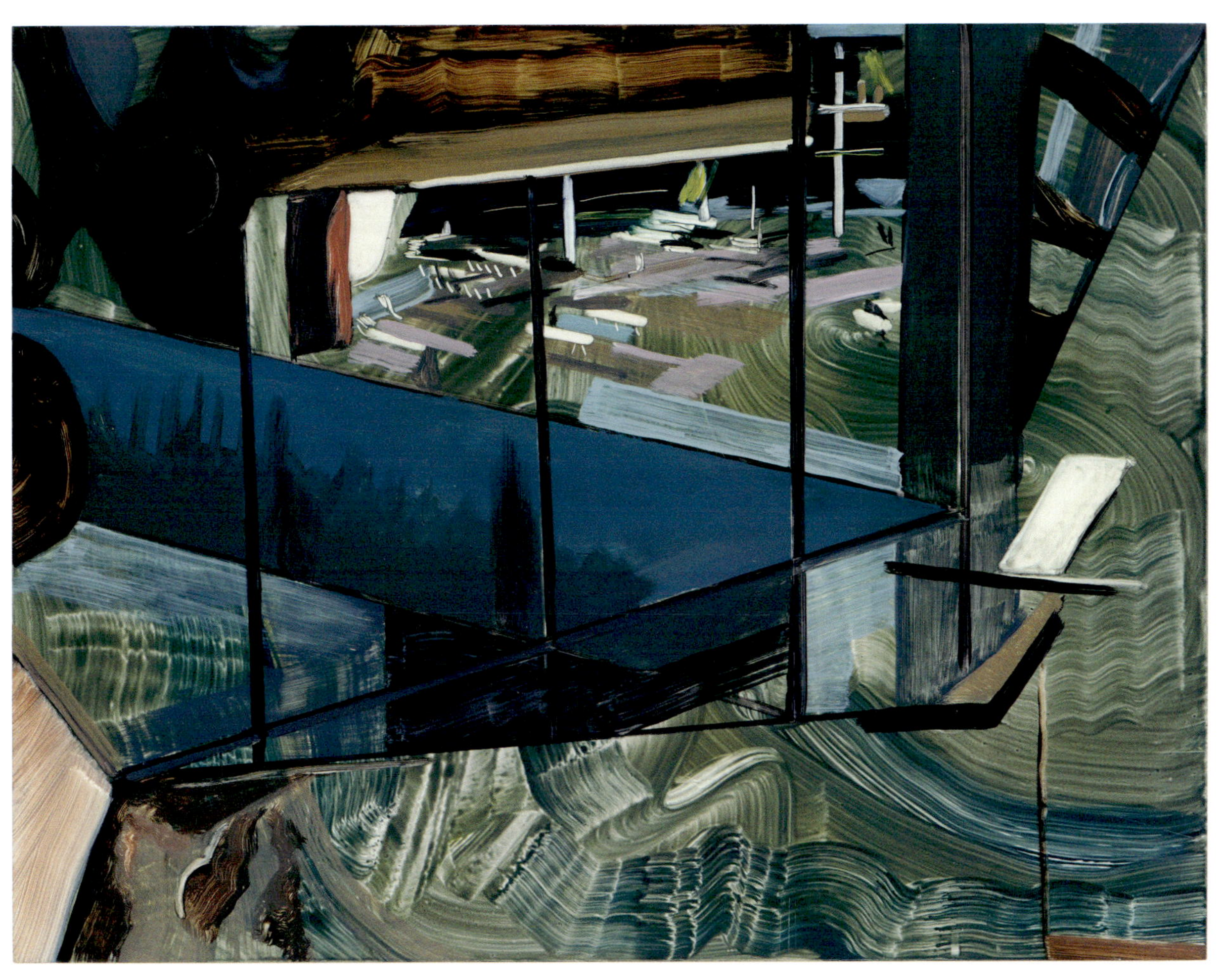

Build Up, 2013, oil on board, 40 × 52.5 cm

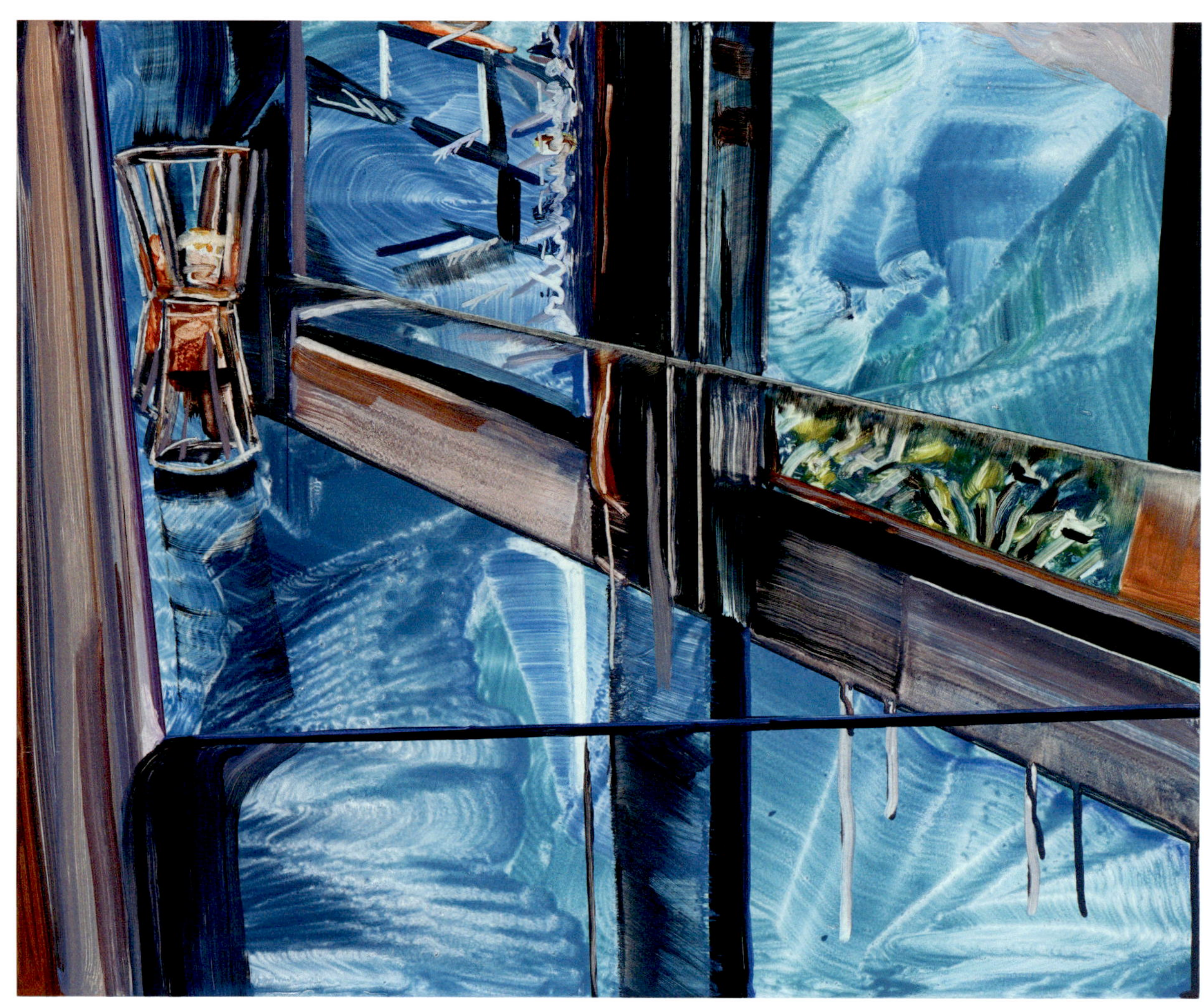

Built Up, 2014, oil on board, 40 × 50 cm

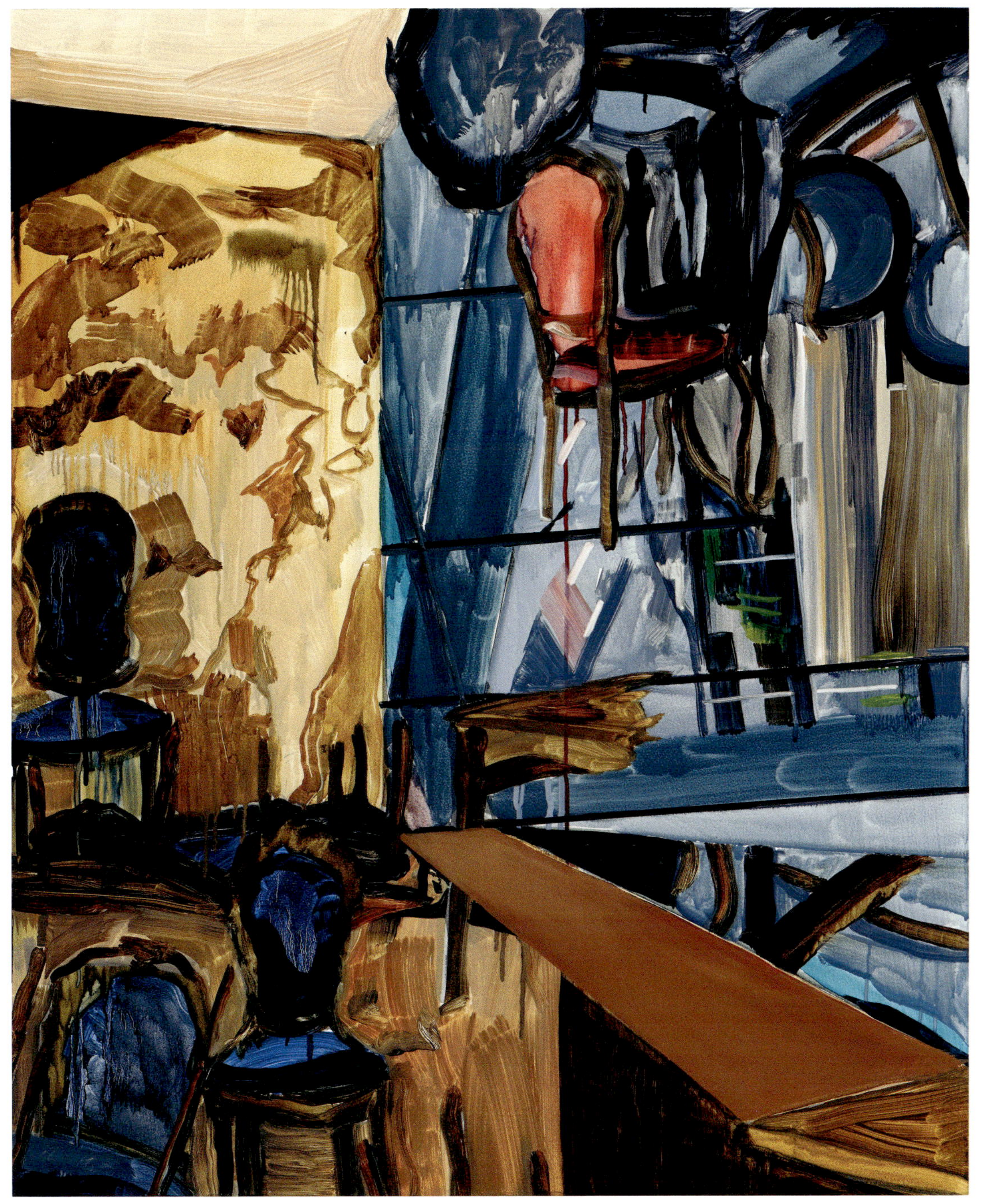

Work Out, 2013, oil on board, 90 × 75 cm

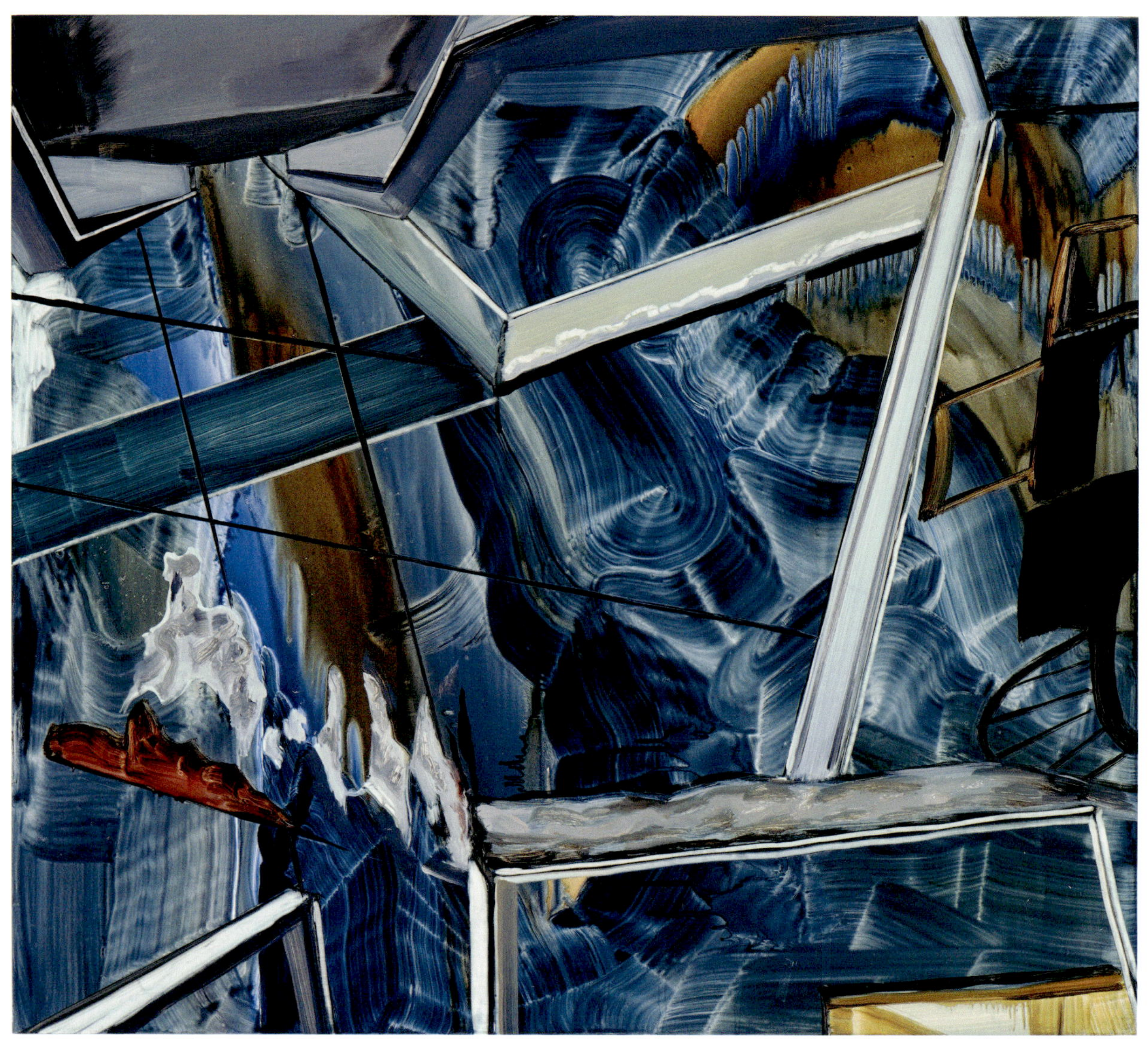

 Composed of a Promise, 2013, oil on board, 65 × 75 cm

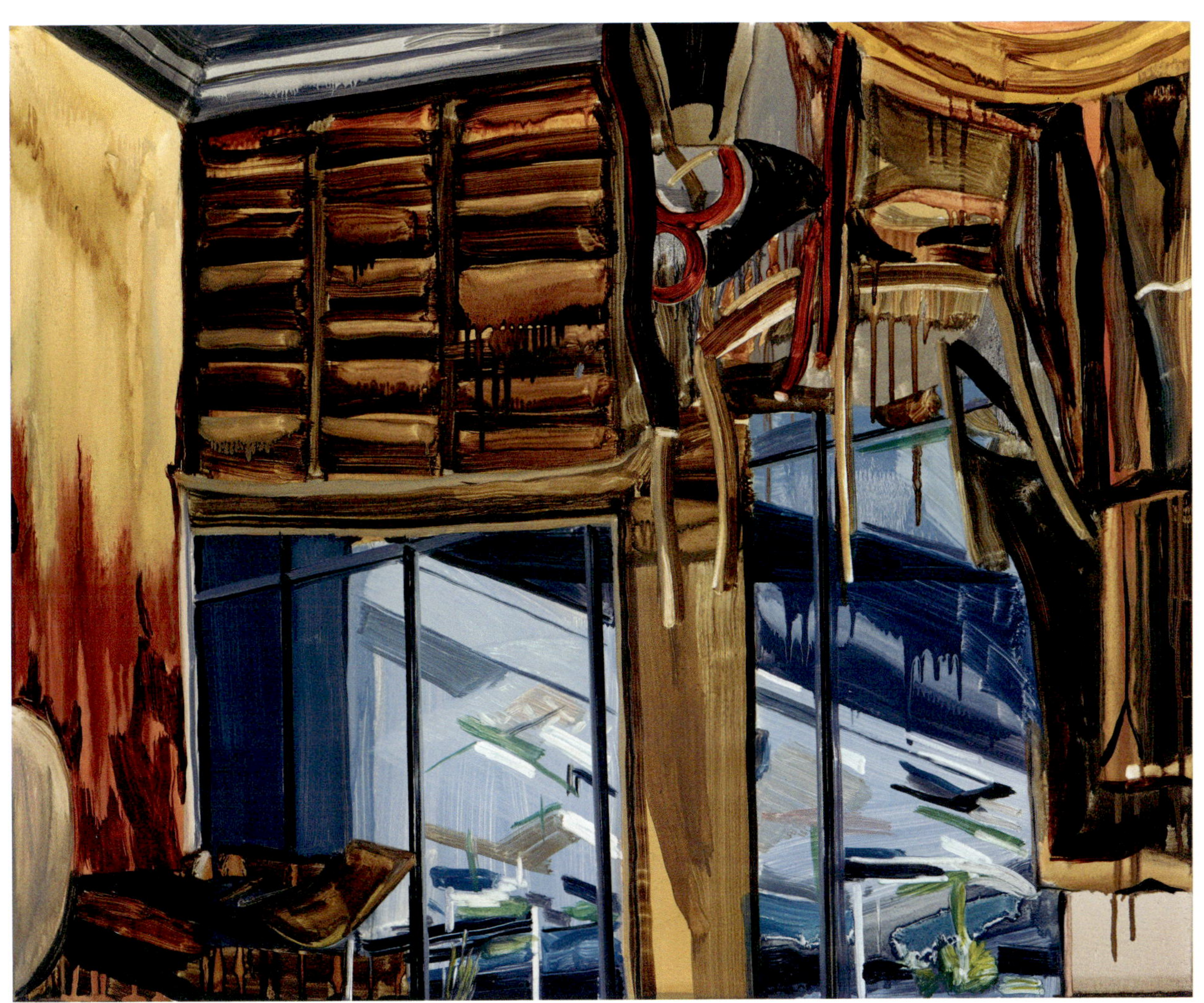

Transitioning, 2013, oil on board, 60 × 75 cm

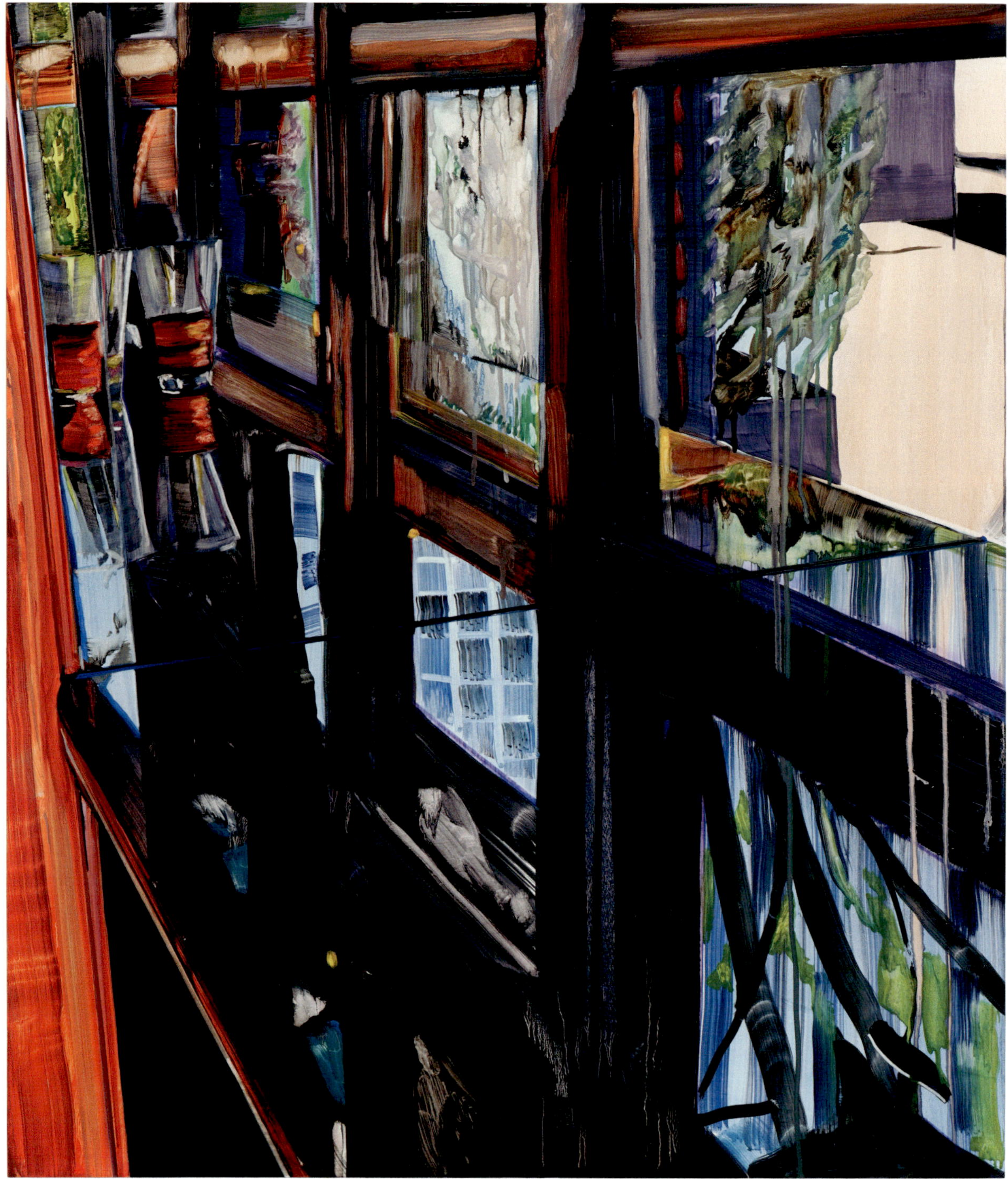

Recharging, 2014, oil on board, 80 × 70 cm

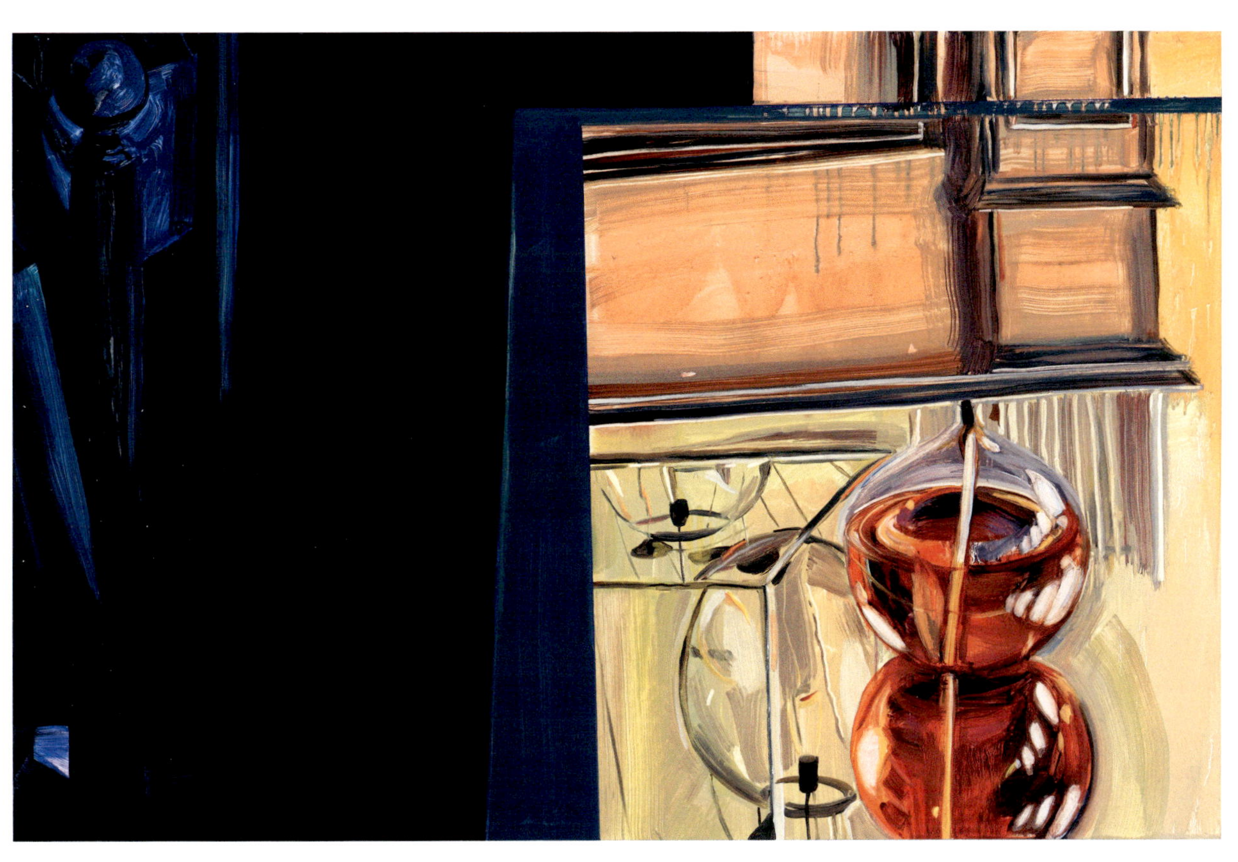

Spliced, 2014, oil on board, 55 × 85 cm

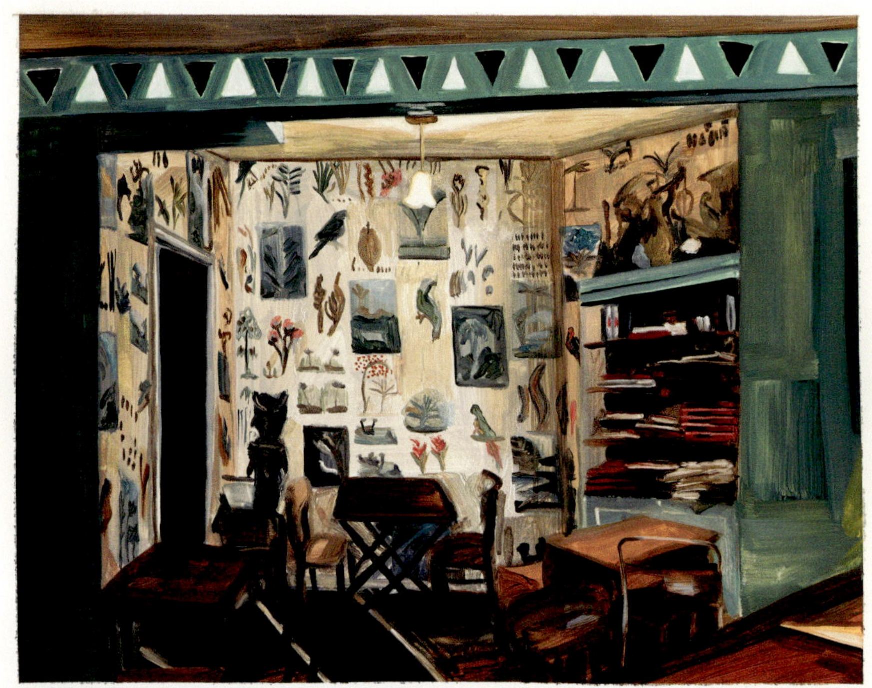

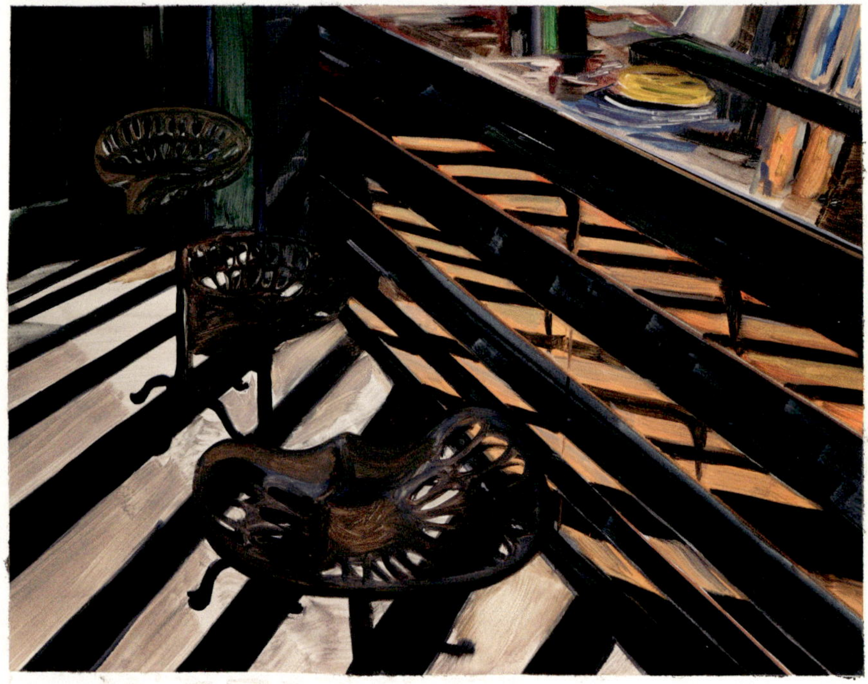

    Social Club, 2014, oil on paper, 48.5 × 62.5 cm   *Stripes*, 2014, oil on paper, 48.5 × 63.5 cm

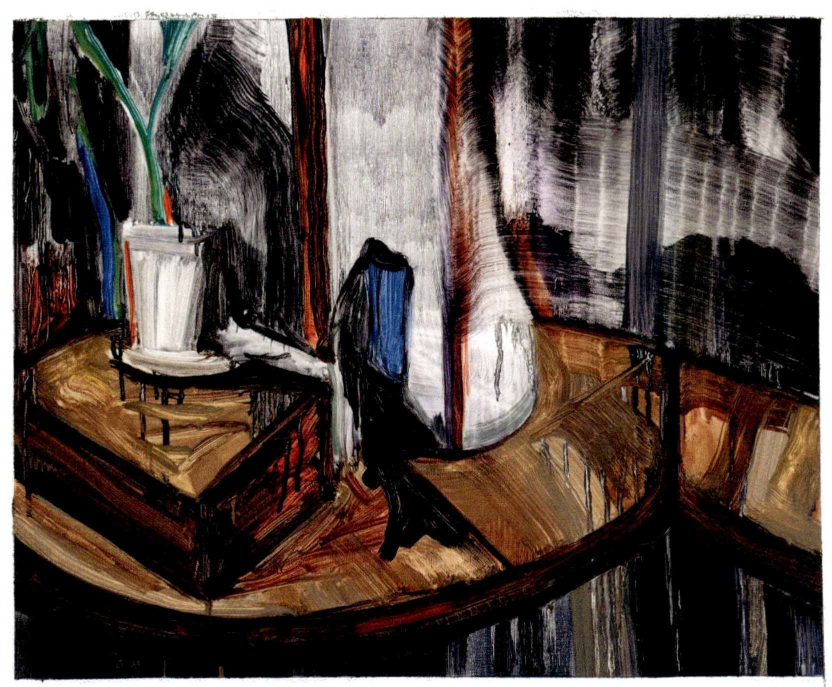

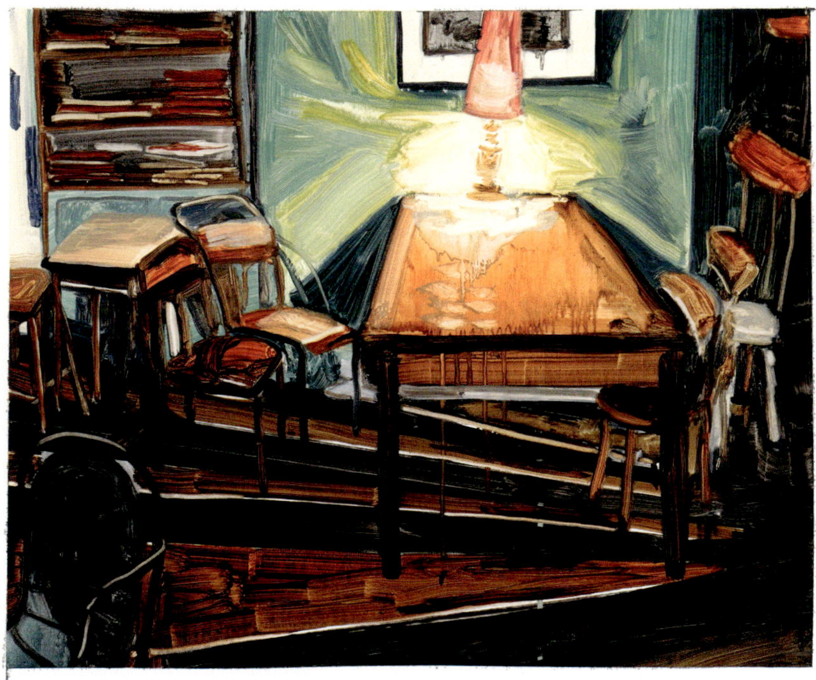

Closing Time, 2014, oil on paper, 39 × 49 cm   *Exposure (After Emmaus)*, 2014, oil on paper, 39 × 49 cm

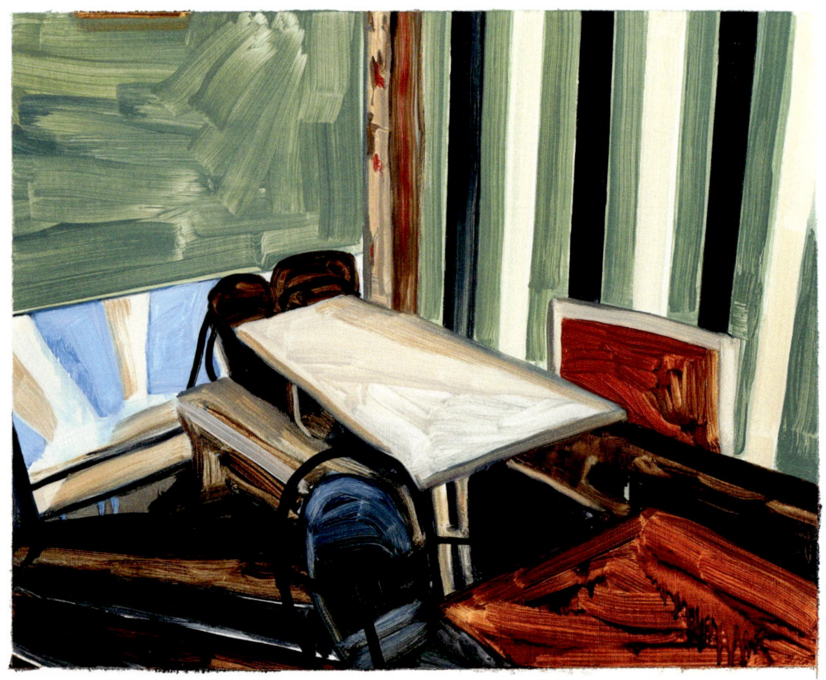

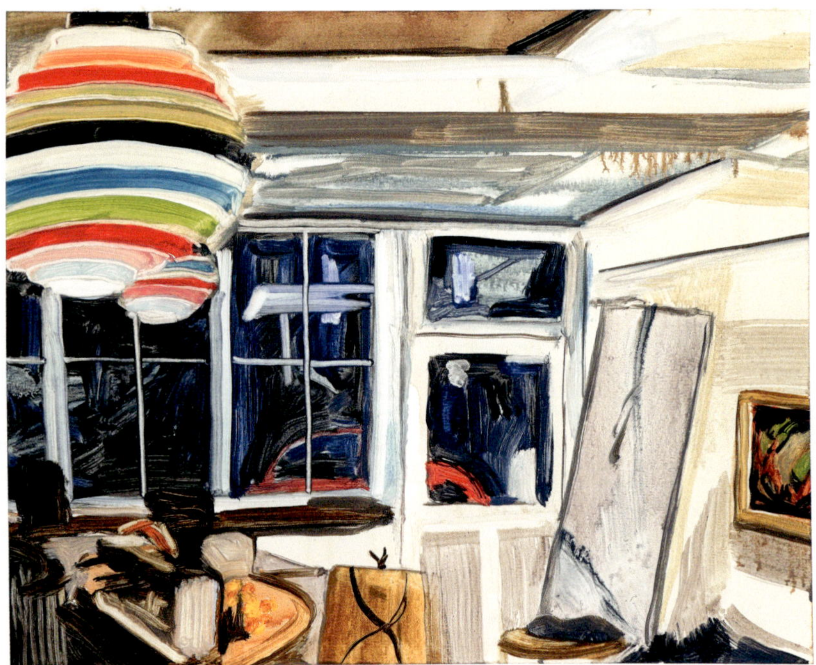

   Shift, 2014, oil on paper, 39 × 49 cm   *The Way Cafe*, 2014, oil on paper, 22 × 27.5 cm

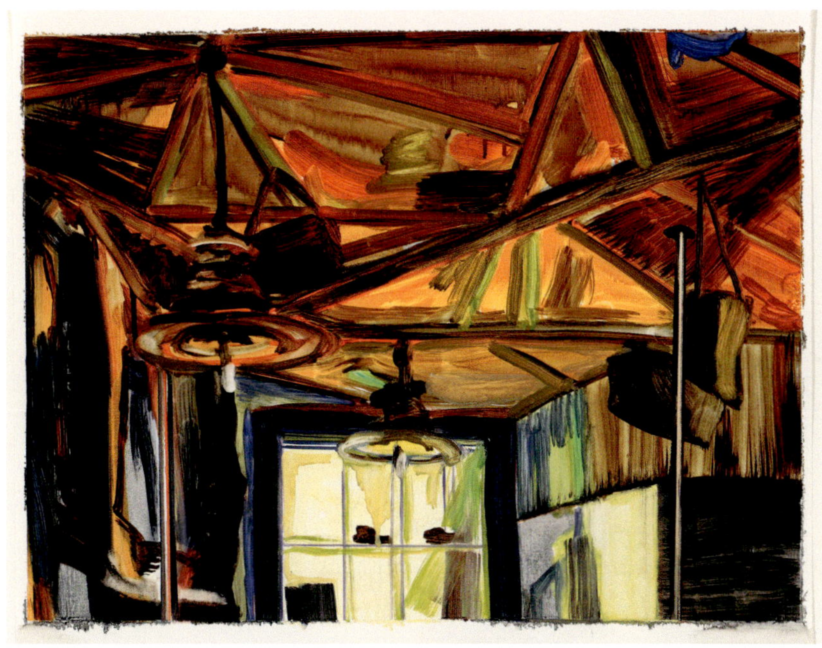

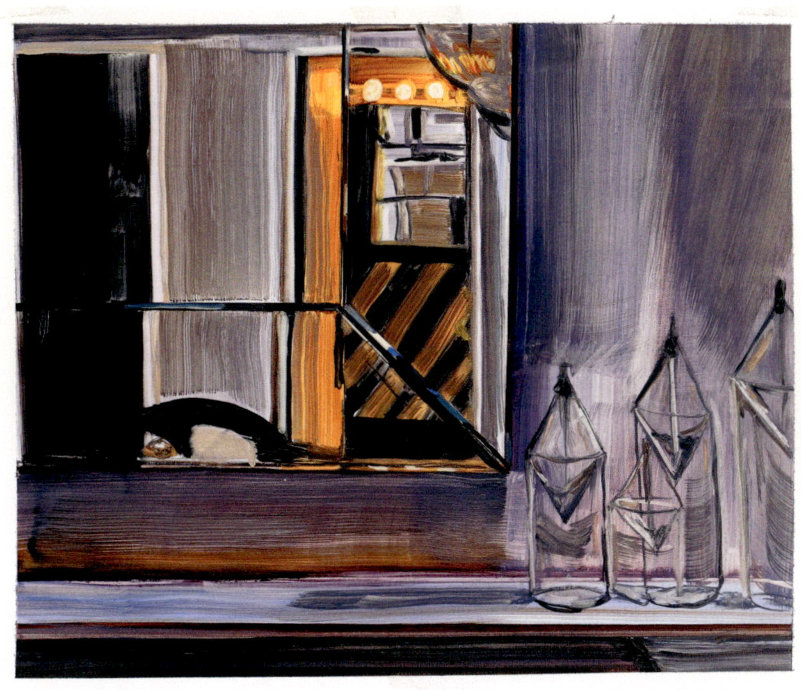

Archive, 2014, oil on paper, 36.5 × 49.5 cm   *Underlying*, 2014, oil on paper, 38.5 × 47.5 cm

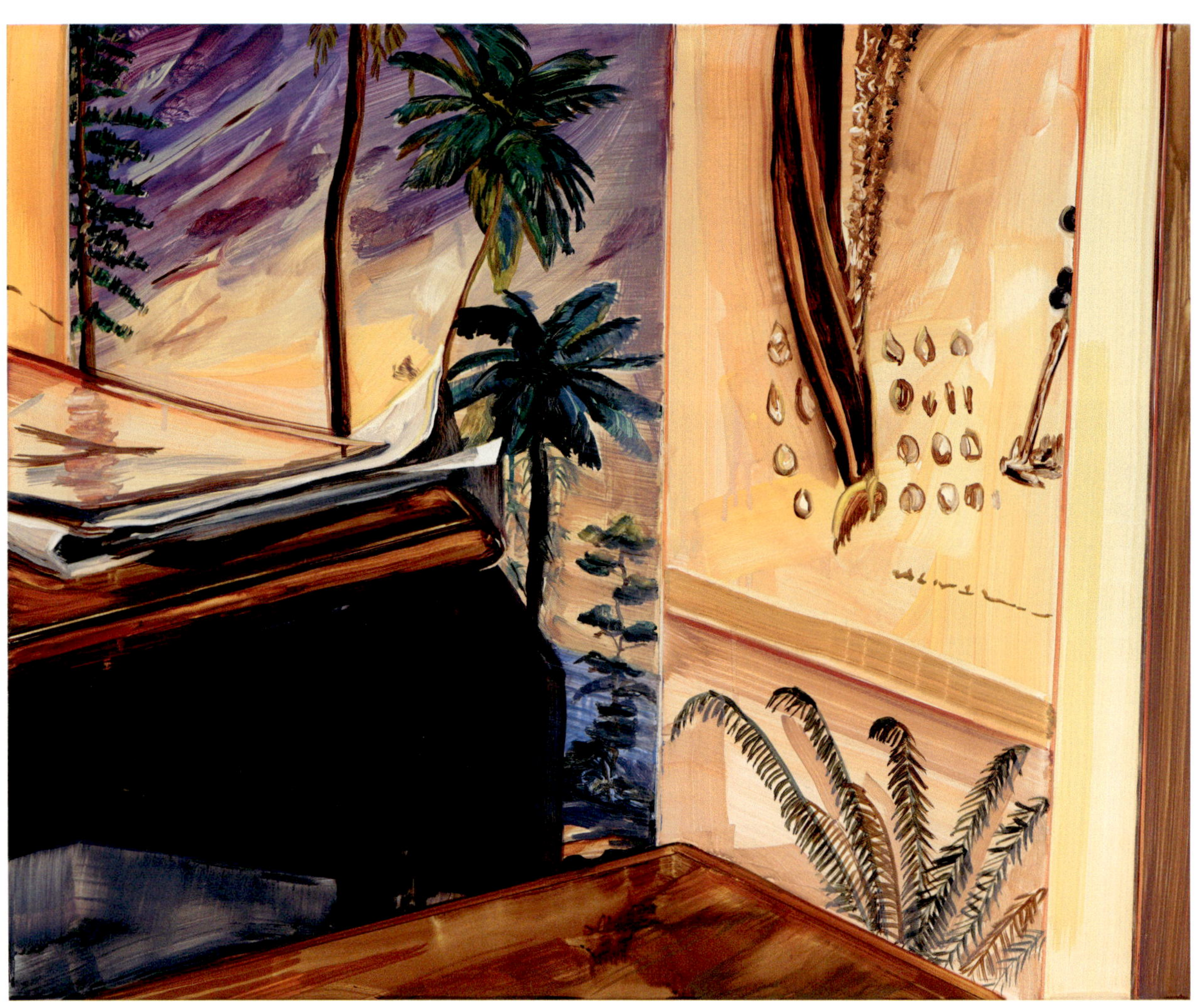

Uproot and Leave, 2014, oil on board, 60 × 70 cm

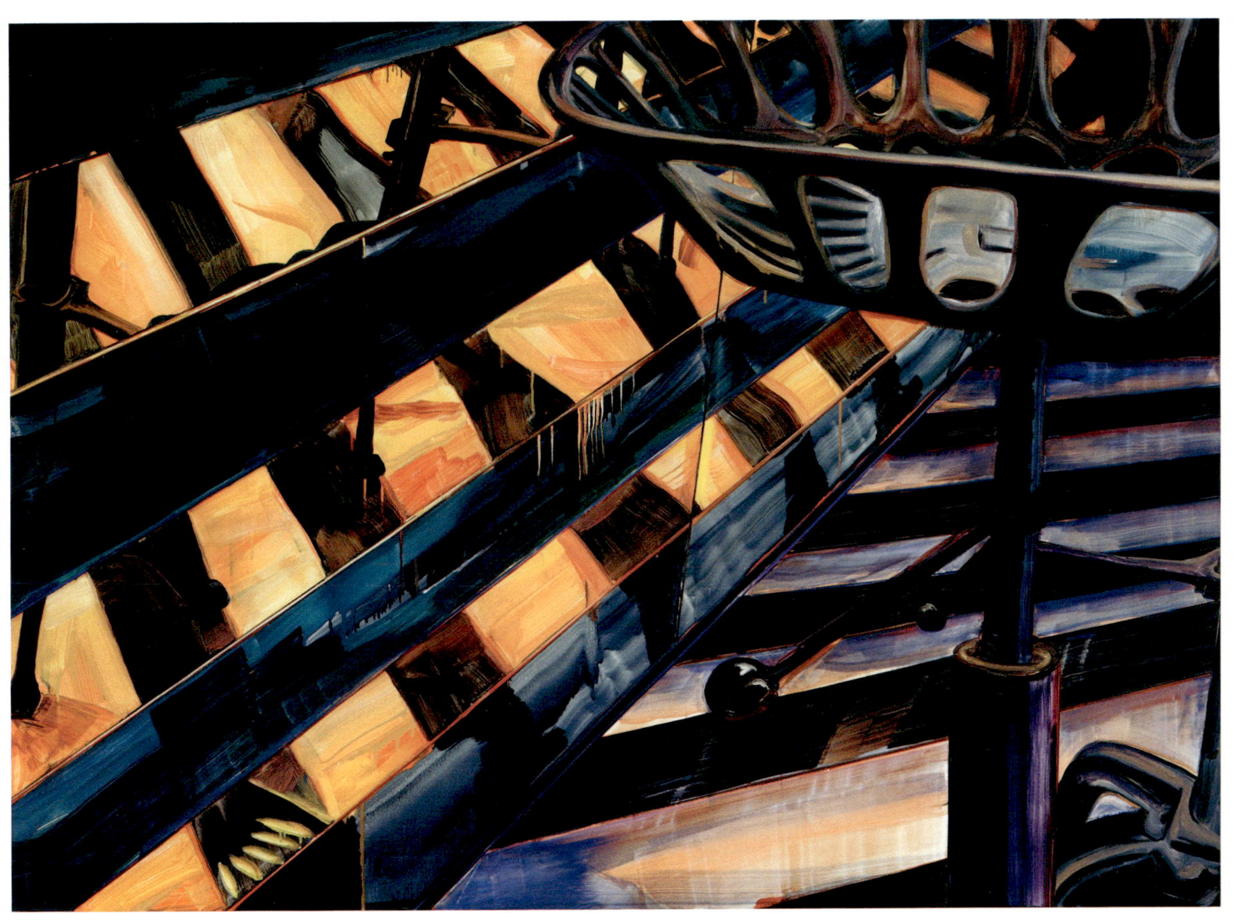

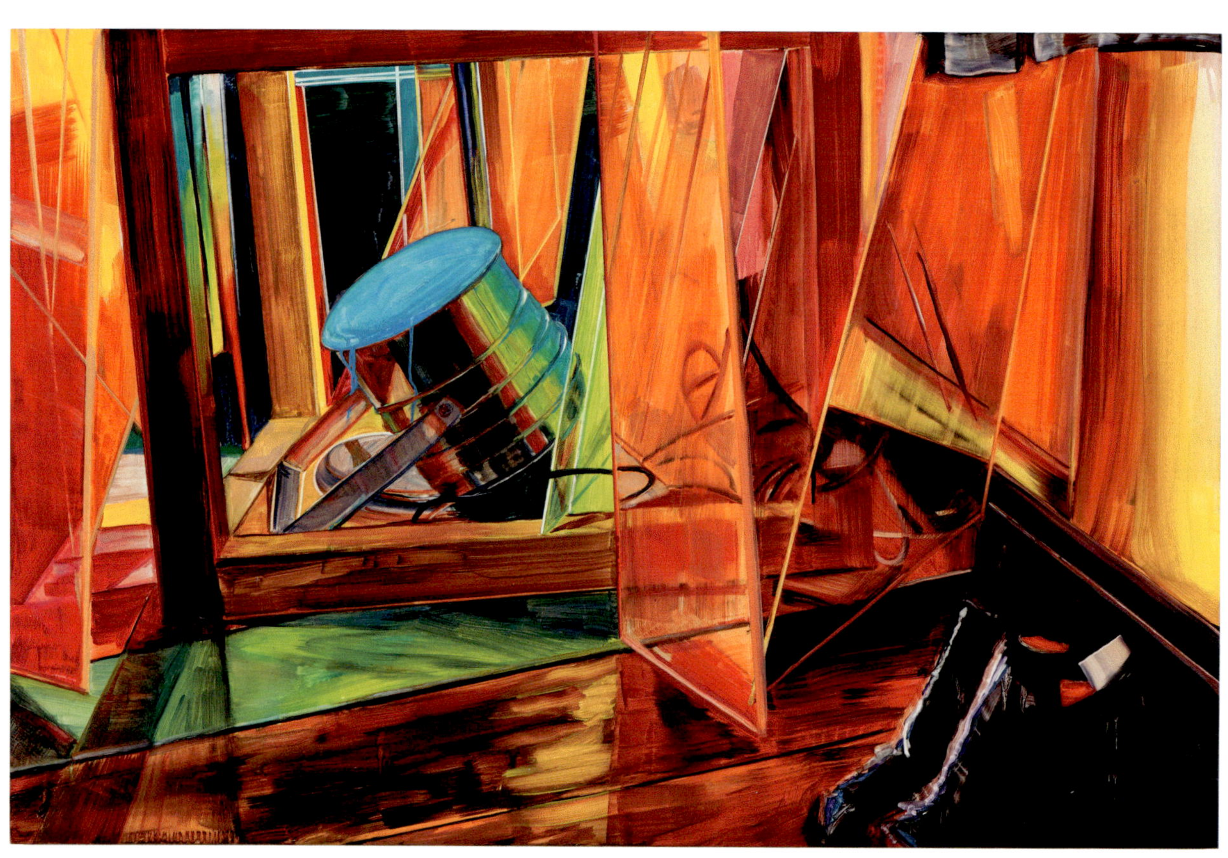

An Awakening, 2014, oil on board, 80 × 122 cm

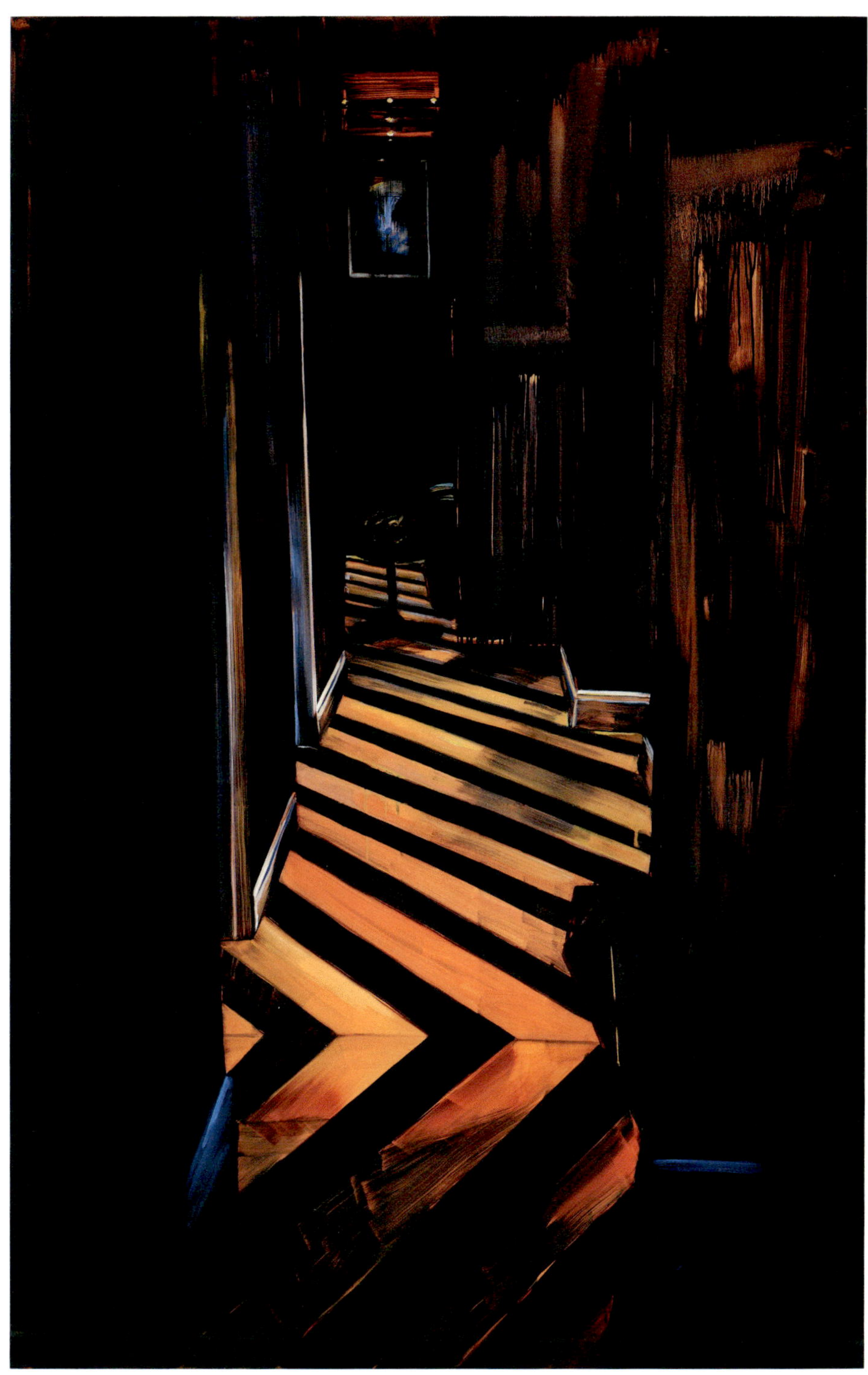

Lodge, 2014, oil on board, 180 × 117 cm

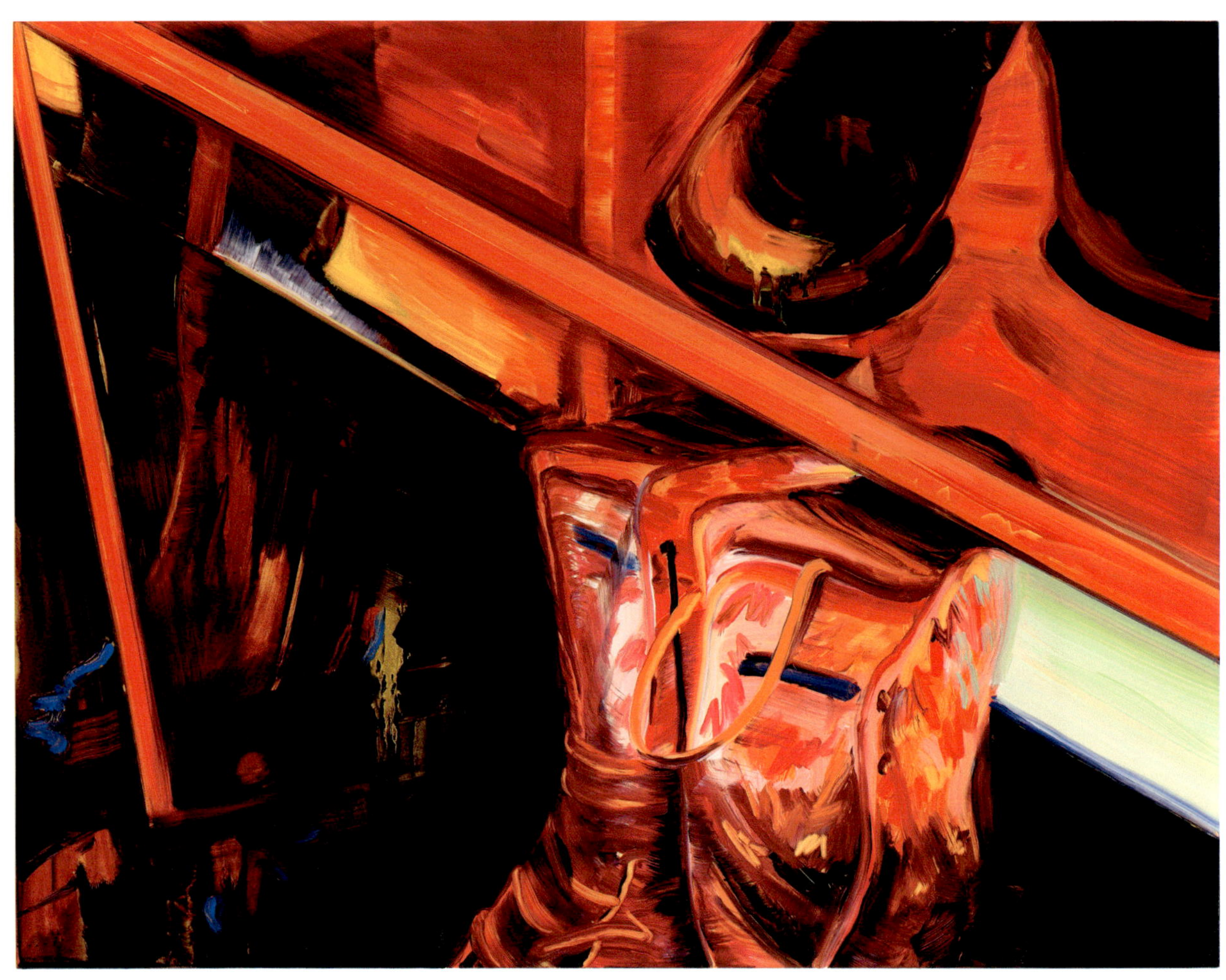

    As Planned, 2014, oil on board, 40 × 52.5 cm

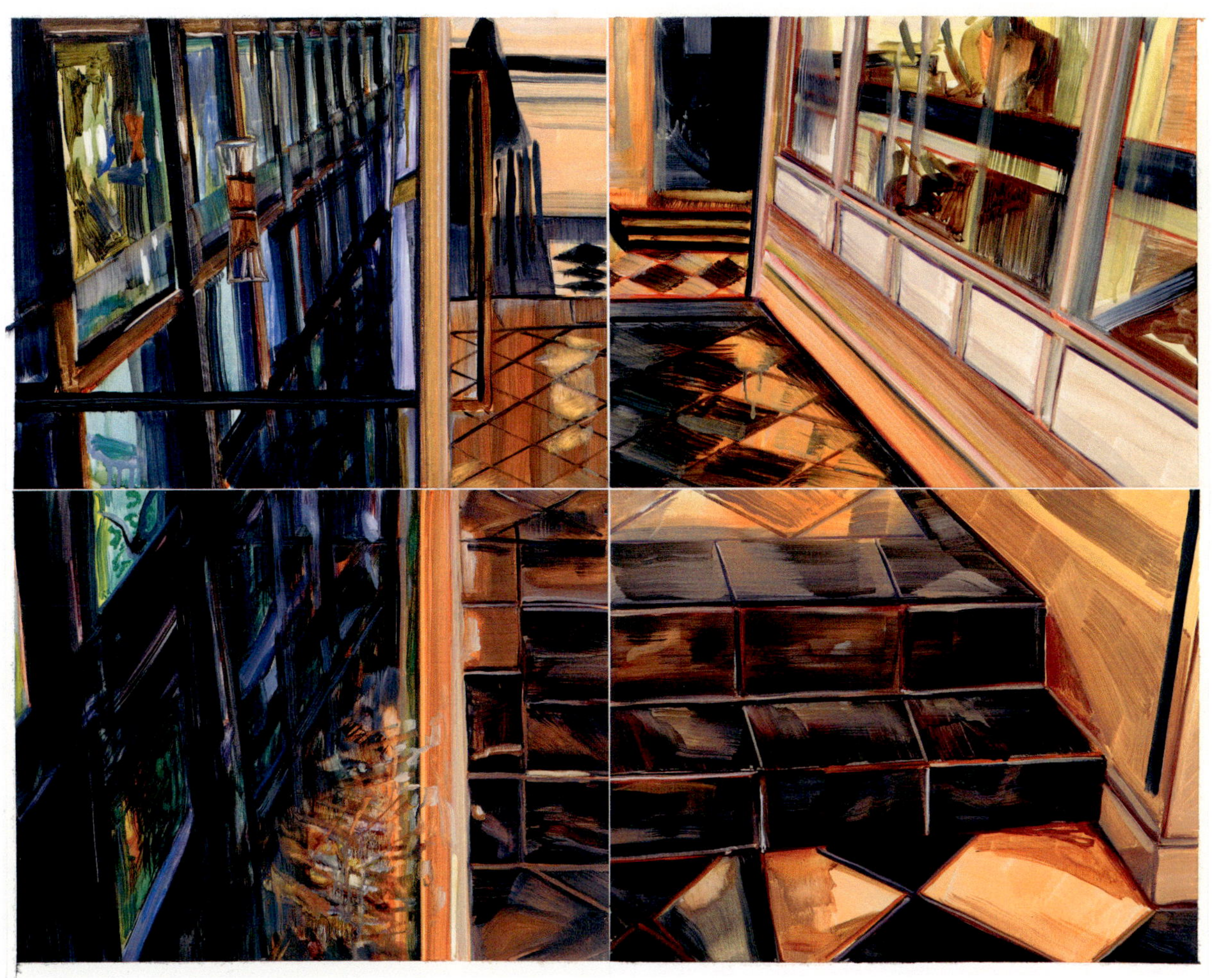

Retreat, 2014, oil on 4 sheets of paper, 78 × 98 cm (total)

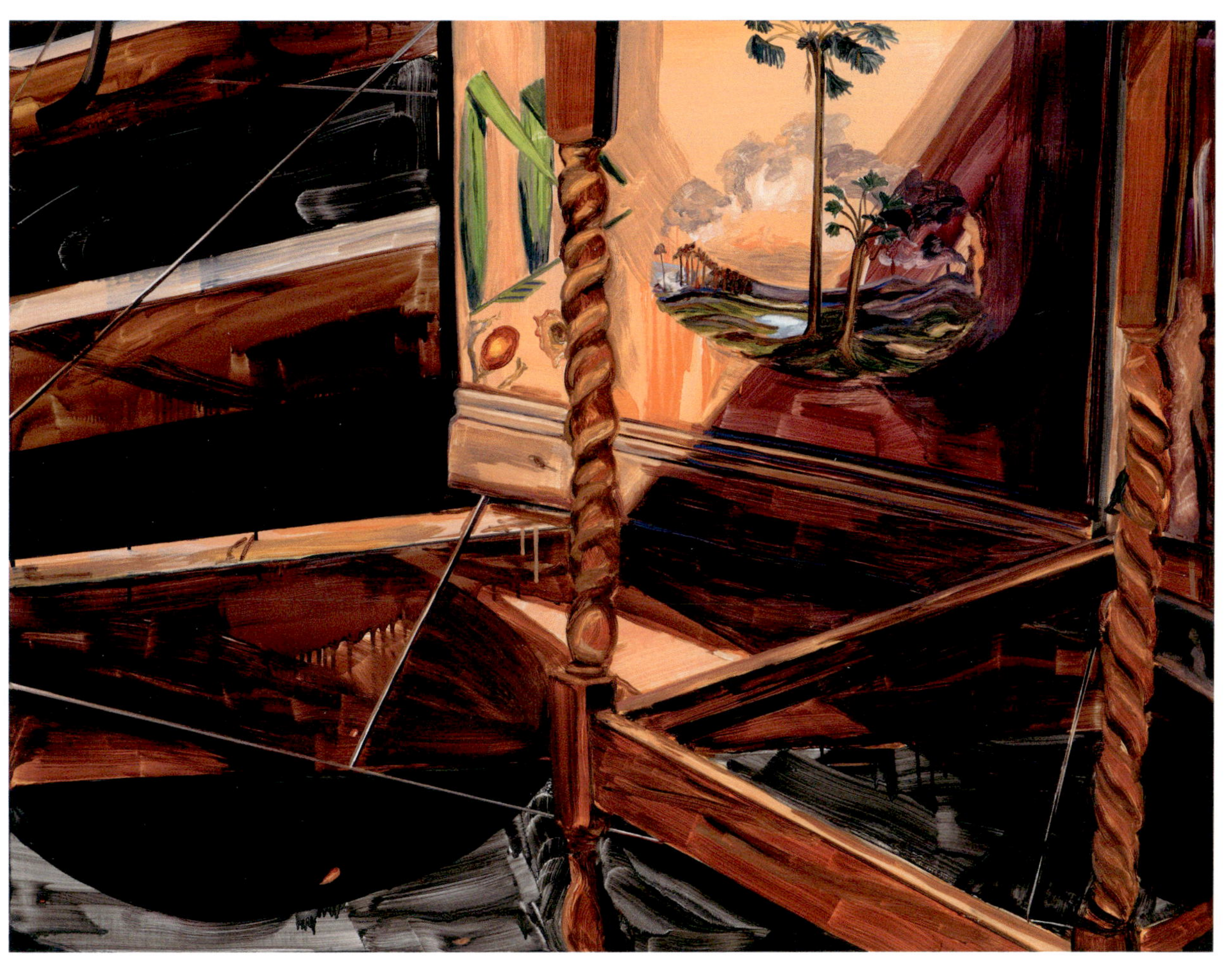

Mobility and Grandeur, 2014, oil on board, 90 × 120 cm

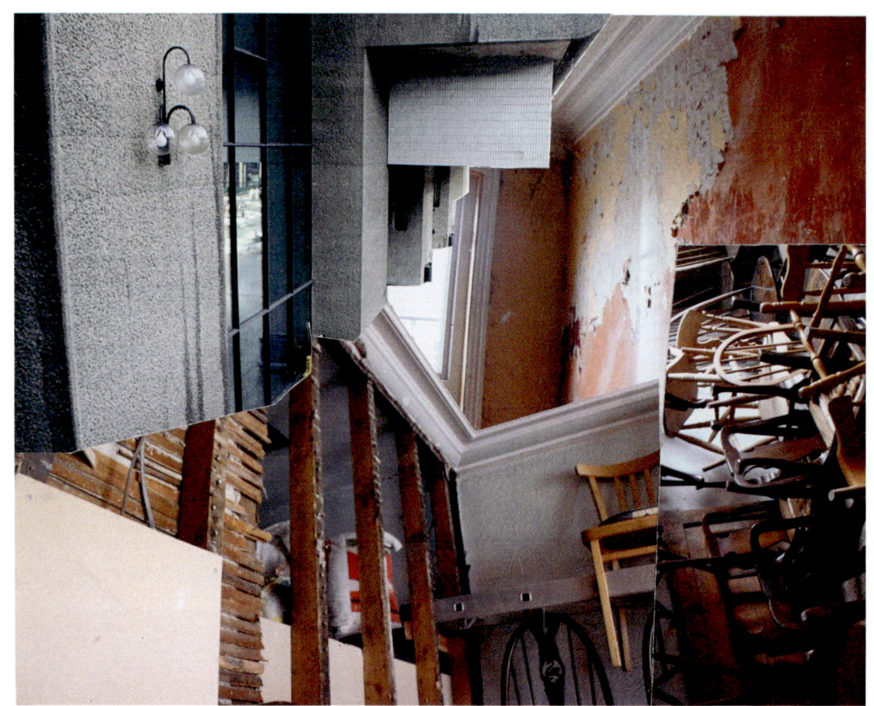

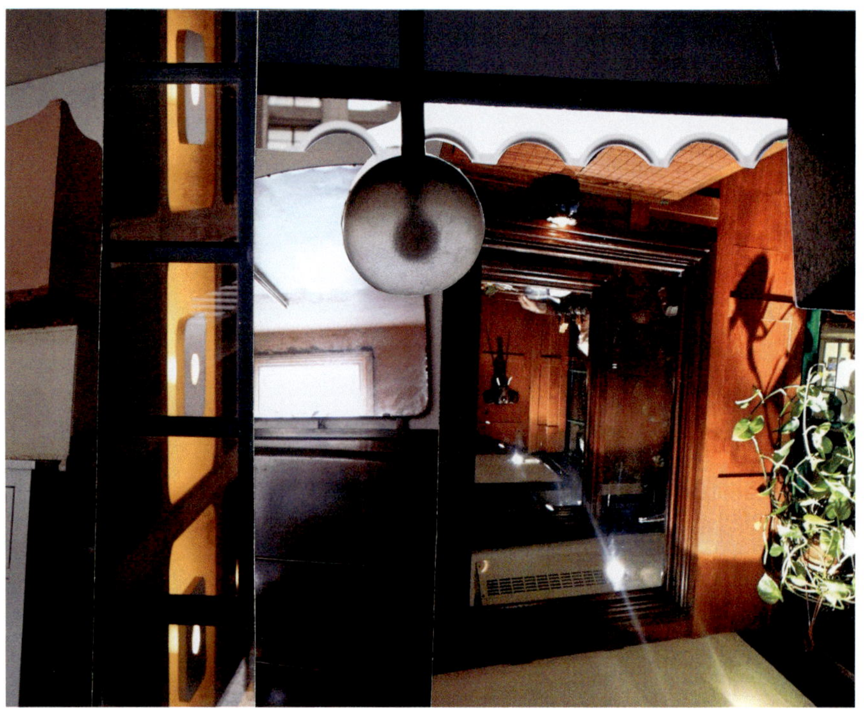

    Untitled (Concrete), 2013, collage on paper, 21.5 × 26.5 cm   *Untitled (Elephant)*, 2013, collage on paper, 20 × 25.5 cm

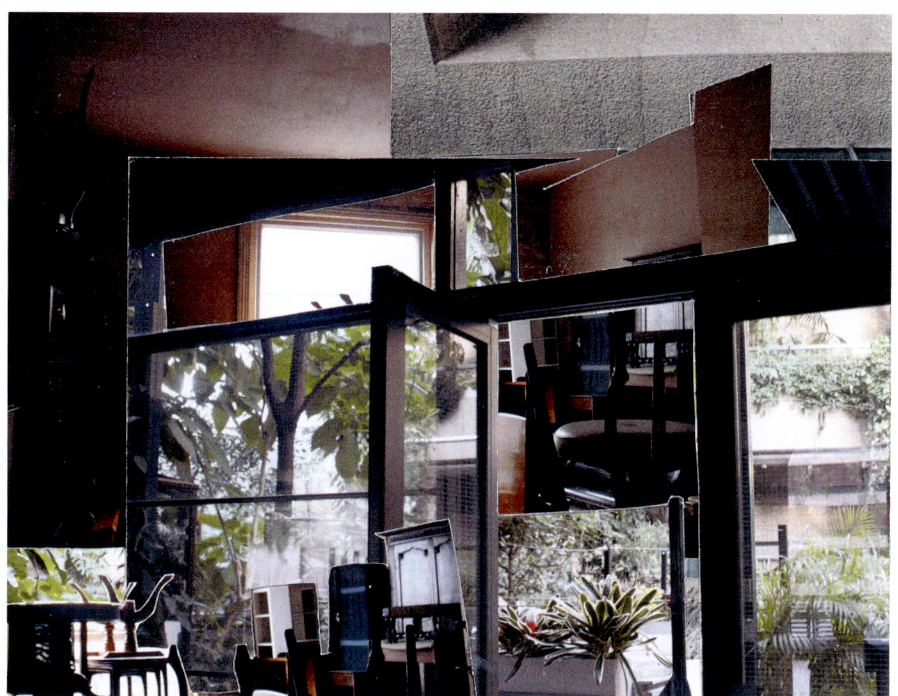

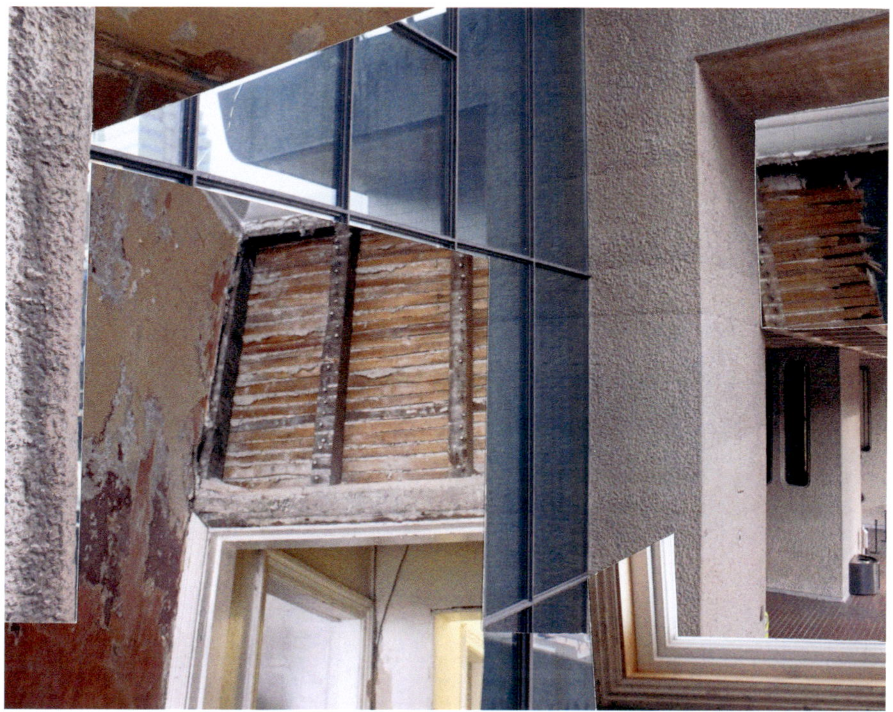

Untitled (Vegetation), 2013, collage on paper, 17.5 × 23.5 cm   *Untitled (Triangle)*, 2013, collage on paper, 15.5 × 20 cm   95

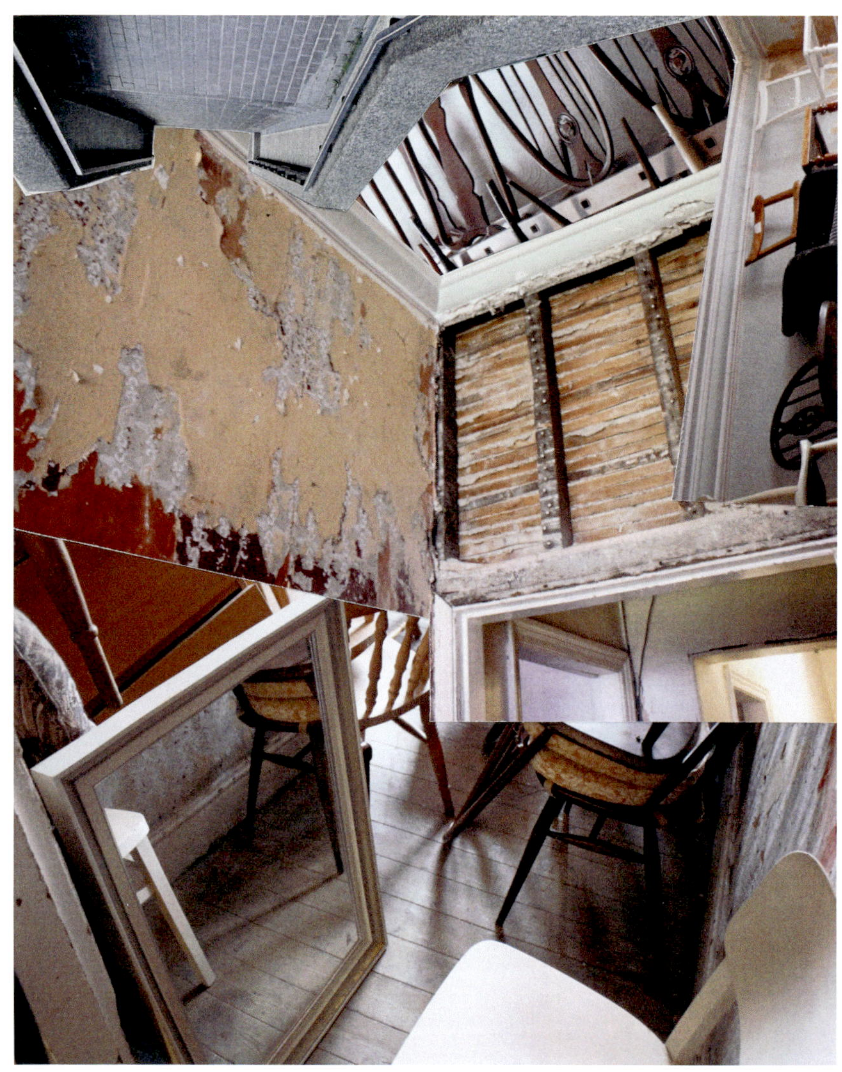

96   *Untitled (Disorienting)*, 2013, collage on paper, 24.5 × 20 cm

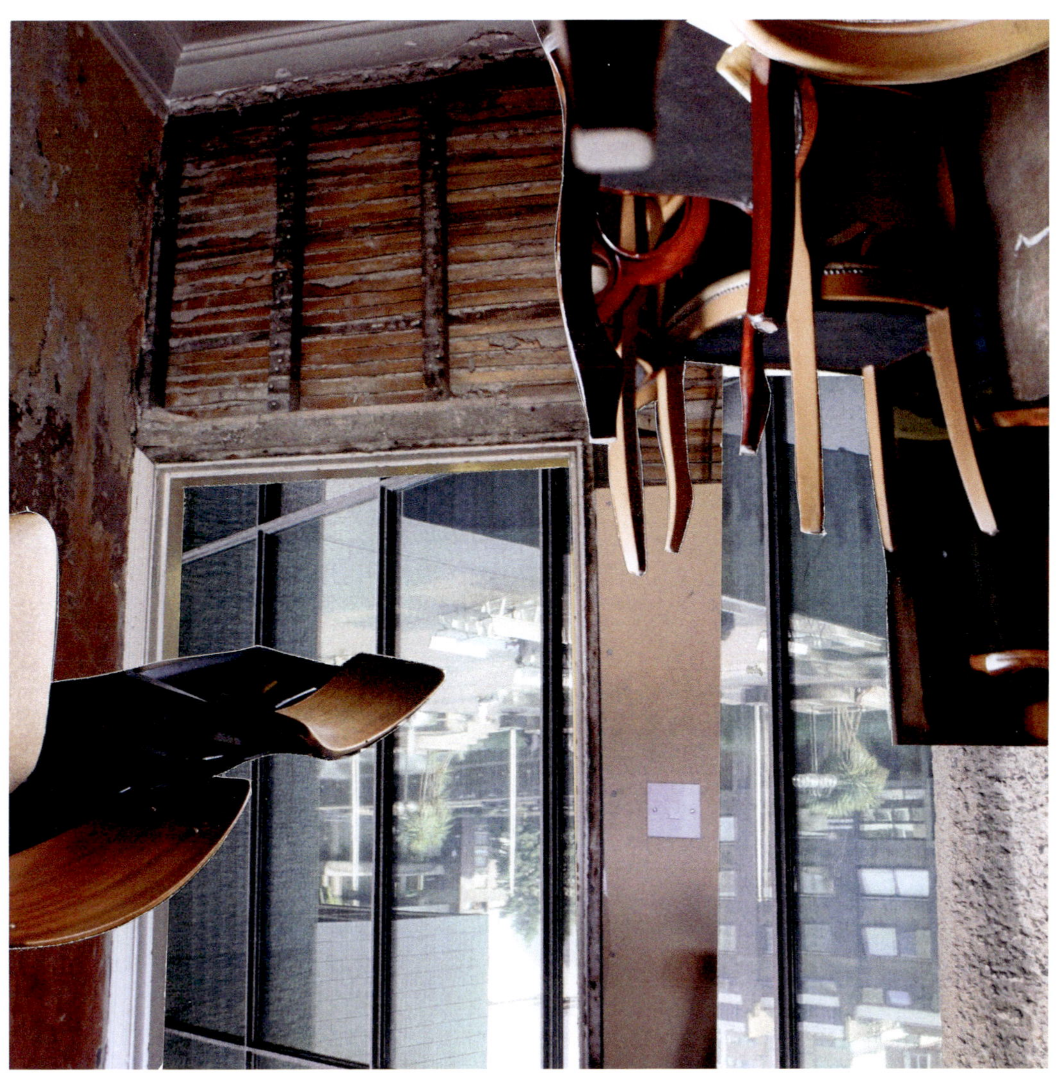

Untitled (Transitioning), 2013, collage on paper, 20 × 20.5 cm

Colophon

Edited by Matt Price
Proofreading by William Lambie
Designed by Joe Gilmore / Qubik

Photography:
Sara Ekholm: pages 2-3, 45-47, 49, 50-53
Gustavo Valdes: pages 12, 16, 18, 35, 38-39, 55-61, 63-71, 73
Rowan Durrant: pages 19, 24-26
Anna Arca: pages 6, 9, 11, 14, 17, 21-22, 28, 31, 33, 37, 44, 72, 75-91, 93-97

Cover image:
Detail of *Mobility and Grandeur*, 2014, oil on board, 90 × 120 cm / reproduced in full on page 93.

First published in 2015 by Anomie Publishing, Wakefield and London
www.anomie-publishing.com

© 2015 Anomie Publishing
All works © 2015 Anna Freeman Bentley
All texts © 2015 their respective authors

A catalogue record for this book is available from the British Library

ISBN: 978-1-910221-03-7

Printed by Pression

Distributed by Casemate Publishers and Book Distributors, LLC, and Casemate UK

Artist's Acknowledgements

I would like to thank Howard and Roberta Ahmanson, of Fieldstead and Company, who funded this book, for their friendship, generosity and support – their enthusiasm, encouragement and delight in God's creation is infectious, sharpening and inspiring; the ever patient David Moore and all at Pied à Terre for supporting the launch of this book and for teaching me the fine art of fine dining; Matt Price and Ben Quash, who have both worked beyond the call of duty; and my husband, Philip Freeman Bentley for his tireless proofing, down-to-the-last-detail questioning and for being a support to me in every way. I love exploring the built environment with you and considering the city that is to come. Finally, I want to dedicate this book to my mother, Julia, and my late father, Ralph Anthony Freeman.

Supported by:

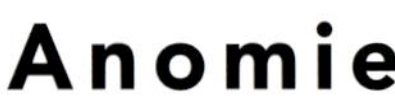 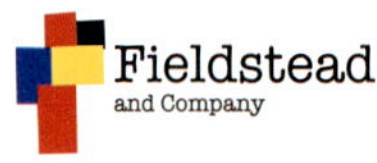 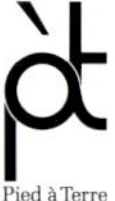